DATE DUE

AP 21 '98	DE 16 03		
MY 14 '98			
JY 31 '99			
DE 11 98			
AR 17 '99			
AP 29 99			
AG 5 '99			
NO 22 99			
AP 29 00			
OC 23 01			
AP 28 '03			

CHOPIN

AMS PRESS
NEW YORK

The Master Musicians

CHOPIN

by

J. CUTHBERT HADDEN

Illustrated

London   *J. M. Dent and Sons Ltd.*
New York   *E. P. Dutton and Co. Inc.*

Publication Data

14.

Reprint of the 1934 ed. published by Dent, London, in
series: The Master musicians.
    Bibliography: p.
    Includes index.
    1. Chopin, Fryderyk Franciszek, 1810-1849. 2. Com-
posers—Poland—Biography. I. Series: The Master
musicians.
ML410.C54H2   1977   786.1'092'4 [B]   74-24094
ISBN 0-404-12939-0

Reprinted from the edition of 1934, London and New York
First AMS edition published in 1977
Manufactured in the United States of America

AMS PRESS INC.
NEW YORK, N.Y.

PREFACE

THE leading authority for Chopin's life is Professor Frederick Niecks's biography in two volumes. Karasowski's life, also in two volumes, is valuable chiefly for letters and other material obtained from Chopin's relatives. It is written without literary skill and disfigured by many uncritical embellishments. Liszt's so-called biography is not a biography at all, but rather a *symphonie funèbre*. James Huneker's *Chopin: The Man and his Music* is excellent for its analysis of Chopin's compositions. Charles Willeby's *Frederic François Chopin*, though less penetrating, is nevertheless to be counted among the important works in English dealing with the composer. The best of the shorter studies is Sir W. H. Hadow's 'Frederick Chopin' in *Studies in Modern Music*. To all these writers I am much indebted, to the last and to James Huneker especially. I have purposely avoided the sentimental gush which has been so largely written about Chopin, and have rigidly confined myself to facts. For the rest, I have endeavoured to tell the story of Chopin's life simply and directly, to give a clear picture of the man, and to discuss the composer without trenching on the ground of the formalist.

J. C. H.

EDINBURGH,
    October 1903.

NOTE TO THE REVISED EDITION

THE late J. Cuthbert Hadden's book on Chopin required less revision than his other volume contributed to this series —on Haydn. His facts were found to be remarkably accurate on the whole, and although the bibliography, which will be found in Appendix D, had to be enlarged by a number of works published since 1903, the literature at the author's disposal at that time has not been swelled by anything that adds materially to our knowledge of Chopin. Also, while the list of Haydn's works has been greatly modified since Cuthbert Hadden wrote his book on that master, and even now remains far from definitive, that of Chopin's compositions has remained substantially as he found it.

The one new source I have constantly kept in view is the collection of Chopin's letters, which, by the way, is now much more easily accessible than it was thirty-one years ago. But even there I found that my labour was more often confirmation than correction.

As in the case of the same author's other volume, I have somewhat tightened and sobered his style, chiefly by reducing his often rather far-fetched literary allusions. My few additions will be found to take the form either of signed footnotes or of interpolations in square brackets, though I did not think it necessary to draw attention to numerous minor interferences. Let the credit for these go to the author, whose work richly deserves such consideration for having remained reliable enough after all these years to call for very few drastic alterations.

E. B.

1934.

CONTENTS

LIST OF ILLUSTRATIONS

CHAPTER I

ONE of Shelley's biographers mourns the fate of 'mighty poets whose dawning gave the promise of a glorious day, but who passed from earth while yet the light in them was crescent.' Shelley, Keats, Byron—these were all extinguished when their powers were still in the ascendant—when their 'swift and fair creations' were issuing like worlds from an archangel's hand. The cant against which Carlyle fulminated so fiercely would fain have us believe that a 'wise purpose' lies behind this untimely slaying of genius. But what if Sophocles had been cut off before the composition of *Œdipus*? Supposing Handel had died before he had begun to think of writing oratorios—before in his fifty-sixth year he conceived the oratorio of *The Messiah*? What if Milton had been known only by the poems of his youth, with no *Paradise Lost* to serve as a treasure for countless poetical descendants? If Burns had lived as long as Goethe or Wordsworth; if Mozart and Schubert had seen Bach's sixty-five summers; if Marlowe had attained the age of Shakespeare; if Raphael had all but touched the nineties like Michelangelo—if all this had been the order of a 'wise purpose,' what splendid achievements the world might now be rejoicing in! No doubt there are cases in which an earlier death would have prevented disastrous mistakes; but I am not with those who regard a man's life as necessarily complete at whatever age he dies. It is an insanity of optimism to delude ourselves with the notion that we possess the best possible works of genius consigned to the grave before its time. When genius is shown by fate for one brief moment and withdrawn before its spring has merged into the fruitful fullness of summer, we must simply, as the biographer of Shelley says, bow in silence to the law of waste that rules inscrutably in nature.

These reflections have a special application in the case of at least four of the great composers. Schubert died when he was thirty-one, Mozart died when he was thirty-five, Mendelssohn died when he was thirty-eight, and Chopin died when he was thirty-nine. Probably Mendelssohn and Mozart, alone of the quartet, with longer lives, would have equalled without surpassing the works which we possess from their pens. On the other hand, Schubert's achievement can hardly be regarded as complete; while in the case of Chopin it is at least reasonable to assume that length of years, extending, let us say, to the Davidic limit of threescore and ten, would have strengthened and expanded his genius and resulted in a series of works which would have secured him a place among the composers whose names we are accustomed to distinguish by the epithet 'great.' But these are vain speculations. As has been well observed, life, in all true reckoning, is counted not by years but by actions. Chopin's life was brief, but it failed not of its purpose.

The exact date of Frederic[1] Chopin's birth, like many incidents of his career, has occasioned some controversy. 'All the foreign biographers of Chopin,' says Karasowski, 'have mistaken the date of his birth. Even on his monument at

---

[1] Fryderyk in Polish.

Père Lachaise in Paris, 1810 is engraven instead of 1809, an error which ought to have been rectified long ago.' If Chopin had indeed been born in 1809 the event would have added one more notable name to the birthday list of that *annus mirabilis* which witnessed the advent of Mendelssohn, Tennyson, Gladstone, Darwin, Oliver Wendell Holmes, Elizabeth Barrett Browning, Abraham Lincoln and Edgar Allan Poe.

But it is not true that Chopin was born in 1809. That year was given by his sister to Karasowski, and it was adopted by Frederick Niecks, who in 1878 was assured by Liszt of its correctness. It is, too, the year which appears on the memorial in the church of the Holy Cross at Warsaw, where Chopin's heart is preserved. There is, however, no documentary evidence in favour of 1809. The short and simple way of settling the point would have been for the biographers to procure a copy of the baptismal certificate; but no one seems to have thought of doing this until the search was undertaken by Natalie Janotha, the well-known Polish pianist.

It is now definitely established that the composer was born on 22nd February 1810, and baptized on 23rd April following. The baptismal certificate found in the records of Brochów Church, Zelazowa Wola, runs, in an English translation: 'I, the above, have performed the ceremony of baptizing in water a boy with the double name Frederic Francis, born on the 22nd day of February, son of the musician Nicolai Choppen, a Frenchman, and Justina de Krzyzanowska, his lawful spouse. Godparents: the musician Franciscus Grembeki and Donna Anna Skarbekowa, Countess of Zelazowa Wola.'

It may seem curious that the term 'musician' should have been applied to the father and the godfather in the

3

baptismal register; but Natalie Janotha[1] explains that the reading of 'musicus' (musician) is an error. The certificate, it seems, has the abbreviation 'Maf.,' which stands for 'Mag-nifico,' the equivalent of our 'Esquire' or the German *Wohlgeboren.*

The father, Nicholas Chopin, appears to have been an interesting personality. He was born in 1771, at Nancy, in Lorraine [but was not, as A. Szulc, the author of a Polish book on Chopin, says, the natural son of a Polish nobleman, who, having accompanied King Stanislas to Lorraine, adopted there the name of Chopin, possibly from the Polish Szop. It has now been established by M. Edouard Ganche that he was the legitimate son of a French wheelwright, François Chopin[2]]. But Nicholas Chopin was a man of education and refinement. He went to Warsaw during the political agitation of 1787 as cashier or book-keeper to a French tobacco manufacturer. His plan to return to France having been frustrated by illness, he was still in the capital when the revolution of which Kosciuszko was the hero broke out in 1794, and shortly after this, having begun to look upon Poland as his second home, he joined the National Guard and bore an active share in the defence of the country. After the fall of Warsaw he again resolved to go to France, but was taken ill once more. Perhaps he saw in this the guiding hand of Providence; at any rate he remained in Warsaw, giving lessons in French.

In 1800 he drifted to Zelazowa Wola, a village not far from Warsaw. He found there a congenial occupation as tutor to the Countess Skarbek's son Frederic, after whom the future composer was named. It was here that he met and

[1] *Athenæum,* 9th February 1901.
[2] See William Murdoch, *Chopin: his Life,* p. 5.—E. B.

4

fell in love with Justina Krzyzanowska, whom he married
2nd June 1806. Justina was born of poor but noble parents.
George Sand declared that she was Chopin's 'only love.'
In one of his own letters Chopin calls her the 'best of mothers.'
She seems to have been an ideal mother—a woman of strong
common sense, of a gentle disposition, and, in her days of
widowhood, given to piety and prayer. One describes her
as 'bright, active and tender-hearted, full of folk-lore and
household recipes, sincere in religion, charitable in conduct,
gentle and courteous in speech.' A Scottish lady who had
seen her in her old age spoke of her to Niecks as 'a neat,
quiet, intelligent old lady, whose alertness contrasted strongly
with the languor of her son, who had not a shadow of energy
in him.' Of course, this was said of Chopin in his later
years. In earlier life he could be, as we shall see, even
feverishly energetic.

Justina bore her husband four children—three girls and a
boy, the subject of the present memoir. Ludwika, the eldest
child, who developed a literary talent, married Professor
Jedrzejewicz in 1832 and died in 1855 at the age of forty-
eight. Isabella, the second daughter, married a school
inspector named Barczinski; while Emilia, the youngest
daughter (Chopin's favourite), who gave evidence of pre-
mature intellectual development, was cut off in 1827 when
she was only fourteen.

The contemporary Brontë sisters and their brother Branwell
occur to one in contemplating this Chopin family of three
girls and a boy—only, however, as regards the comparatively
early deaths and the fact that chest trouble was at work in
both households. The Chopin girls were certainly not
Brontës, for, though they seem to have had the temperament
of genius, they had none of its accomplishments; and Chopin

himself was as far as possible from resembling the *habitué* of Haworth's 'Black Bull,' who wanted to die, as Hadrian said a Roman imperator should do, standing. Whence the divine fire that came into these families was derived by way of heredity is a question beyond conjecture, for the mental faculties of the parents were in neither case unusual. We can only say of Chopin and Charlotte Brontë what Walton says of the poet and the angler—they were 'born to be so.' They illustrate no theory of the origin of genius.

Nicholas Chopin's career subsequent to the birth of his son may be briefly outlined. In 1810 he returned to Warsaw, and was appointed Professor of French at the newly founded Lyceum. This post he retained for twenty-one years, having meanwhile added to his duties by undertaking the French professorship at the School of Artillery and Military Engineering (1812) and at the Military Elementary School (1815). For a number of years, too, he kept a boarding school, which was patronized by some of the best families in the country. [Among his pupils there were Titus Woyciechowski, Juljan Fontana and the brothers Anton and Felix Wodzinski, who remained Frederic's intimate friends.] Nicholas Chopin's last appointment was at the Academy for Roman Catholic Clergy. Karasowski says that the failure of his physical powers was much hastened by the strenuous exertions which he had undertaken on behalf of his adopted country, and adds that his declining years, which he spent in retirement and in the enjoyment of a pension, were beclouded by anxiety about his son. His death took place in 1844 at the age of seventy-four. His wife survived him by fifteen years, having seen all her family but one consigned to the grave.

Chopin, it will thus be gathered, was peculiarly fortunate in his parents and early associates. With a French scholar for a father, a Polish mother rich in all true womanly virtues, and a trio of clever sisters always ready to pet him, the boy grew up, like Mendelssohn, in an atmosphere of charming simplicity, love and refinement. He seems to have been from the first something of a weakling. Sir Henry Hadow calls him 'a little frail, delicate elf of a boy,' which is a fair description. Liszt says that he was 'fragile and sickly,' and that 'the attention of his family was concentrated upon his health.' He took no interest in outdoor sports and exercises, and had none of the usual boyish adventurousness. One can hardly imagine him scaling scaffoldings, like Haydn, or tearing his clothes or getting his feet wet. But he was assuredly not the 'moonstruck, pale, sentimental calf of many biographers.' Karasowski has several tales of his vivacity and love of practical joking: some evidently authentic, others as evidently apocryphal. He played innumerable tricks on his sisters and his school-fellows, and even on persons of riper years. We are told that one afternoon, when the pupils had become unusually boisterous, he restored them to order by improvising romances. That story may be accepted with a very slight hesitation; but the other, which represents him as sending the same unruly youngsters to sleep by representations of night on the piano, must be politely discredited.

It is clear at any rate that his spirits were sufficiently high, perhaps too high for that slender frame, that delicate constitution, in which the seeds of disease were already sown. The birthdays of his parents and friends were frequently celebrated by theatrical representations, and in these he usually took a prominent part. One dramatic artist said that on account of his presence of mind, his excellent declamation and his capacity for rapid facial changes, Chopin was born to be a great actor. Balzac and George Sand shared this

7

view, which receives some further support from the fact of his having collaborated with his sister Emilia in the writing of a comedy. The comedy was, we may be sure, as little noteworthy as Master Samuel Johnson's reputed verses to his duck, but Chopin's share in it may at least be taken as an evidence of his juvenile interests and activities.

It is, of course, not uncommon to find high spirits and love of fun coexisting with a delicate and refined sensibility. The case of Charles Lamb instantly occurs to one—the prince of practical jokers, and yet sensitive in the highest degree. I have heard of a boy of six, cheerful, healthy, high-spirited, rushing out of the room in which Sir Arthur Somervell's music to *The Forsaken Merman* was being played. He was found sobbing in another apartment. 'I will not listen to it!' was all he could say. So it was with Chopin. We read that when quite a child he 'wept whenever he heard music and was with difficulty restrained.' One unsympathetic biographer compares this with the 'responsive howls' of a dog when an instrument is played. It is rather an indication of susceptibility, partly physical, partly mental, and prepares us for the early interest in music which Chopin showed. He was no baby composer, writing scores and extemporizing sonatas and concertos before he had cut his first tooth. But he took to the piano almost as soon as he could walk—as if, in short, it were by natural destiny. His parents, being sensible people, resolved to do all that was possible to foster his evident talent. A master was engaged for him in the person of Adalbert Zywny, a Bohemian, who played the violin and taught the piano. Hadow, arguing from the fact that in after life Chopin's system of fingering was entirely original and unorthodox, conjectures that Zywny never really showed him how to play a scale. The inference loses some of its point from the fact that Chopin devised a system of fingering for himself, a system arising out of the peculiar demands of his own music. There is a tradition that Zywny allowed the boy to spend most of his time in improvisation. However that may be, he gave his young pupil a thorough grounding in the rudiments of his art, encouraged and guided his talent for extemporizing, and so advanced his progress at the key-board that before long he became the wonder of all the drawing-rooms of Warsaw.

Frederic Chopin, in fact, was in some danger of developing into that unnatural product of modern exploitation known as the 'infant prodigy.' A Polish lady who heard him play when he was not quite nine wrote of him as a child who, 'in the opinion of connoisseurs of the art, promises to replace Mozart.' Precocious he undoubtedly was, even in an age of such precocity as that of Mendelssohn and Liszt. But he could never have been the *Wunderkind* that Mozart was. For one thing, he had no burning desire to shine in public. Even when he made his first public appearance at a charity concert on 24th February 1818 in a concerto by Gyrowetz, it was not his own achievement that interested him most: it was his personal appearance. He had been dressed in a new jacket with a handsome collar for the occasion; and when the anxious mother, who had stayed at home, asked him what the audience liked best, he naïvely replied: 'Oh, mamma, everybody was looking at my lace collar.' Here was the dandy in embryo. Chopin, as Byron said of Campbell the poet, was always 'dressed to sprucery.' This was not from vanity or conceit, as it often is with wearers of long hair and fur-trimmed coats, but merely because it gave him pleasure to have fine, neat clothes, just as it gave him pleasure to have flowers about his room. With all his little affectations, there was not a particle of conceit about Chopin. That is perfectly apparent from his letters. When Angelica Catalani visited Warsaw in 1820 and, impressed with his talent, gave him a watch with a flattering inscription, he appreciated the compliment less than the idea of possessing a new toy.

The influence of his early contact with the *bon ton* of Warsaw on Chopin's tastes and temperament is worth remarking. He always had, as Karasowski puts it, 'an aversion to coarse people, and avoided any one who lacked good manners.' The feeling was probably inborn, and it had certainly been fostered at home, where all sorts of interesting personages were constantly calling, and where, besides, he was always coming in contact with his father's pupils. But with the flower of the Polish aristocracy vying with each other in their patronage of the young musician, it was only natural that elegant sur-roundings should become to him a sort of second nature and give him that impress of an aristocrat which, in the days of his fame, no one who came near him failed to note. The Polish biographer's pages devoted to this part of his career are peppered with the names of society grandees in whose salons he was eagerly welcomed—Czartoryskis, Radziwills, Lubeckis, Skarbeks, Pruszaks, Hussarzewskis, and the rest. He was introduced to the Princess Lowicka, the unhappy wife of that typical Russian bear the Grand Duke Constan-tine, and frequently improvised in her drawing-room. He had fallen into the habit of casting his eyes towards the ceiling when engaged in these visionary exercises, and one day the duke remarked to him: 'Why do you always look upwards, boy? Do you see notes up there?' What did Chopin not see 'up there'?

[It was for the grand duke that Chopin, in 1820, wrote a march. The exalted dedicatee had it arranged for military band, played in public and published; but, perhaps because it was scored by somebody else, it appeared without the youthful composer's name.]

Liszt, in his rhapsodical, not to say hysterical book on the composer, has some characteristic gush about these adulatory gatherings.

Chopin [he writes] could easily read the hearts which were attracted to him by friendship and the grace of his youth, and thus was enabled easily to learn of what a strange mixture of leaven and cream of roses, of gunpowder and tears of angels, the poetic ideal of his nation is formed. When his wandering fingers ran over the keys, suddenly touching some moving chords, he could see how the furtive tears coursed down the cheeks of the loving girl or the young neglected wife; how they moistened the eyes of the young men, enamoured of and eager for glory. Can we not fancy some young beauty asking him to play a simple prelude, then, softened by the tones, leaning her rounded arms upon the instrument, to support her dreaming head, while she suffered the young artist to divine in the dewy glitter of her lustrous eyes the song sung by her youthful heart?

Liszt's experiences with women were peculiar. There was nothing to match them in the career of Chopin. The most that can be said about these aristocratic ladies and gentlemen who buzzed about him is that they made life pleasant for the dreamy young genius, and enabled him to lay up a treasure of happy memories against a time when happy memories could be almost his only solace.

For that he was happy now is certain. Some sentimental writers, representing him as a plaintive pessimist, hooting, as Dumas says, at the great drama of existence, have pictured his early life as a mixture of poverty and misery. Nothing could be farther from the truth. Poverty, of course, is a comparative term. But while in his son's babyhood Nicholas Chopin, thanks mainly to Napoleon's rampant militarism, must have experienced something of the worries of straitened resources, things improved greatly after 1815, when the Congress of Vienna established a Kingdom of Poland; and enlargement of means came to the French professor with the gradual restoration of the great families. Chopin's life was singularly free from all the grosser conditions of anxiety; and if health had only been granted him it might have been 'roses, roses all the way.' He never had to pawn his possessions, like Mozart, or sell his manuscripts, like Schubert, before he could order a meal.

The boy having begun to compose in earnest, his father wisely determined to provide him with a master for theory. Here again he made an excellent choice. Joseph Elsner had gone to Poland from his native Silesia in 1792. In 1816, when Chopin was six years old, Elsner established a school for organists in Warsaw, where he was subsequently (1821) entrusted with the direction of the newly founded Conserva-toire. Several of his pupils attained distinction, and the esteem in which he was held by the general public is attested by the handsome monument, raised by subscription, which adorns his tomb in Warsaw.

From what has been recorded of Elsner it is evident that he was just the man to direct the theoretical studies of an original genius like Chopin. He was assuredly no pedant quoting his chilling formulas to check the tendency of his pupil for 'splendid experiments.' When people complained to him of Chopin's airy evasion of certain rules of harmony and counterpoint, he would reply: 'Leave him alone; he does not follow the common way because his talents are uncommon. He does not adhere to the old method because he has one of his own, and his works will reveal an originality hitherto unknown.' When one remembers how some instructors of the great masters hindered and repressed their pupils' efforts to strike out a new path, it is impossible not to feel a measure of sincere regard for Joseph Elsner. Chopin himself entertained for him a lasting love and reverence. When he went to Paris he wrote asking his advice about studying under Kalkbrenner, and the name of the old master continually crops up in his letters. 'From Zywny and Elsner,' he said, 'even the greatest ass must learn something.'

No details have come down to us of Chopin's course of study under Elsner. In a letter of 1834, addressed to Chopin, Elsner refers to himself as 'your teacher of harmony and counterpoint, of little merit, but fortunate.' Karasowski speaks of Chopin's 'profound knowledge of counterpoint,' but Chopin's works nowhere exhibit a profound knowledge of counterpoint in the strict sense. It is doubtful if Elsner himself possessed such a knowledge: those of his compositions which have been examined do not indicate anything of the kind. Some contend that he was too easy-going with Chopin. But he taught him to love Bach; and if he allowed him, for the most part, to take his own course, what then? As one has said, with a conscientious pupil the method of encouragement is the easiest possible way to inculcate a feeling of responsibility, and the most successful teacher is he who knows how to train mediocrity and to leave genius a free hand.

Concurrently, of course, with his theoretical studies Chopin was labouring hard in the improvement of his pianistic technique. He had an instrument in his bedroom and would often get up during the night to do a spell of practice or to try the effect of some particular combination which had been engaging his thoughts. 'The poor young gentleman's mind is affected,' was the compassionate comment of the servants. But Chopin knew very well what he was about. As Charles Willeby remarks, the pianoforte 'school' of that time was totally insufficient for his requirements, and necessity, the mother of invention, led him gradually on to those experiments in tone and technique which so revolutionized the practice of the keyboard and resulted in the development of a new style. Karasowski says that Chopin showed a preference for the organ as offering the widest scope for his improvisations. The assertion seems doubtful in view of the fact that Chopin's genius was so essentially a genius of the piano. Yet one is not so sure. The middle part of the G minor Nocturne (Op. 37, No. 1), for example, looks very organ-like. At any rate Chopin clearly did play the organ. George Sand tells how, on the way home from Majorca in 1839, he took the instrument at the funeral of Adolphe Nourrit, the operatic tenor, who, in a fit of despondency, had thrown himself from a window in Naples. It was at the church of Notre-Dame-du-Mont, in Marseilles. 'What an organ!' writes the novelist. 'A false, screaming instrument which had no wind except for the pur- pose of being out of tune. . . . He, however, made the most of it, taking the least shrill stops, and playing *Les Astres* (Schubert's song, *Die Gestirne*), not in the enthusiastic manner in which Nourrit used to sing it, but plaintively and softly, like the far-off echo from another world.'

This is authentic. The only other reference I have found to Chopin's organ playing is a dubious anecdote told by Sikorski and Karasowski. According to this Chopin some- times sat in the choir and played the organ at the Wizytek Church, which was attended by the students of the Warsaw University. One day, when the celebrant had sung the *Oremus,* Chopin extemporized in an ingenious manner on a motive from the mass just performed. The choristers and band left their places and gathered round the player spell-bound. The priest at the altar complacently awaited the pleasure of the musician, but the sacristan rushed angrily into the choir, exclaiming: 'What the devil are you doing? The priest has twice intoned *per omnia saecula saeculorum*, the minis-trant has rung repeatedly, and still you keep on playing. The superior who sent me is out of all patience.' Poetic imagina-tion has almost certainly been at work on this anecdote, if indeed the whole thing is not an invention.

So far Chopin had been receiving his general education at home among his father's pupils. In 1824 he was sent to the Warsaw Lyceum, where he 'worked hard, rose rapidly, won two or three prizes and gained the esteem and respect of his school-fellows by developing a remarkable talent for carica-ture.' There is a story of his having made an unflattering portrait of the Lyceum director, who, becoming possessed of the sketch, returned it with the sardonic comment that it was excellent! This tendency to caricature the peculiarities of others became, as James Huneker observes, a distinct, ironic note in his character, though in later life the trait was much clarified and spiritualized. Possibly it attracted Heine, though Heine's irony was on a more intellectual plane.

While at the Lyceum, he generally spent his holidays in the country, most frequently at the village of Szafarnia. There, as Karasowski informs us, he conceived the idea of bringing out a manuscript newspaper after the pattern of the *Warsaw Courier*. He called it the *Szafarnia Courier*, and its contents were made to serve in place of the ordinary home letters. Here is one paragraph, showing that even while on holiday he was not wholly divorced from his beloved music. It must be premised that 'M. Pichon' was a name he had

Chopin

assumed. 'On 15th July,' runs the note in the journal, 'M. Pichon appeared at the musical assembly at Szafarnia, at which were present several persons big and little. He played Kalkbrenner's Concerto, but this did not produce such a furore, especially among the youthful hearers, as did the song which he rendered.' This, so far as I am aware, was the only occasion on which Chopin sang, either in public or in private. But perhaps he was indulging in a joke, and did not sing at all! Compare Charles Lamb again: this was just the sort of mystification *he* enjoyed.

The influences of these Szafarnia holidays—the open-air life, the songs of the reapers returning from their labours, the dancing at the harvest homes, and so on—must have made themselves felt, if insensibly, later on when he began to compose in earnest. In a letter to one of his schoolfellows he says:

> I spend my time in a highly agreeable manner. Don't fancy you are the only one who can ride. I too can sit a horse. . . . I ride, that is, I go wherever my steed pleases to take me; clutching at its mane I feel just as comfortable as a monkey would feel on a bear's back. I've had no fall to lament so far, because my steed hasn't yet been inclined to throw me, but I shall fall the first time it takes the fancy. I don't want to fill your head with my affairs. The flies often select for domicile the bridge of my nose, but who cares? It's a custom of these plaguy insects. The midges honour me with their bites. But who cares for this either, as they do at any rate spare my nose?

This is an essentially boyish letter, on which account alone it is interesting.

Of the next few years of his life the details are rather meagre. In 1825 he made two public appearances in Warsaw, the first in May, the second in June, playing Moscheles's Concerto in G minor and improvising as usual. At the earlier concert he had to show off an instrument bearing the portentous name of the Æolopantalon, a sort of combined piano and har‑monium, which had just been invented by Dlugosz of Warsaw.[1]   Later on he played before the Emperor Alexander, who had come to Warsaw to open the parliamentary session, and went from the royal presence with many compliments and the more substantial reward of a diamond ring.   The Rondo in C minor (Op. 1) was composed about this time.

Next year—that is to say in 1826—his parents began to detect signs of over‑study, and he was accordingly packed off, with his sister Emilia—who was in the last stages of consumption [2]—to Reinerz, a watering‑place in Prussian Silesia, to try the effect of the whey cure.   We hear little about the whey, but the rest did him a world of good, and he is soon found writing in the liveliest spirits to his schoolfellow Wilhelm Kolberg.   His musical enterprises seem to have been limited to a charity concert which he got up on behalf of two orphans whose mother had just died, leaving them totally destitute.   Chopin had always a kindly, sympathetic heart.

From Reinerz he went on to Strzyzewo, where he spent the rest of the summer with his godmother, who had become Madame Wiesiolowska.   While there he made a short stay with Prince Anton Radziwill at Antonin, where the dis‑tinguished musical amateur had his country residence.   The prince does not figure prominently in the musical dictionaries; but he was so good a composer that his incidental music for the first part of Goethe's *Faust* was performed for several years at the Berlin Singakademie.   He had an agreeable tenor voice, was a capable cellist and altogether exactly the kind

[1] See Grove's *Dictionary of Music and Musicians,* article 'Æolodion.'
[2] Emilia died on 10th April 1827.

of man in whose company Chopin was likely to find pleasure. Liszt makes the extraordinary statement that he 'bestowed on Chopin the inestimable gift of a good and complete educa' tion.' Another report credits him with defraying the cost of Chopin's tour in Italy. As Chopin never made an Italian tour, that report is easily disposed of: the other is likely to have as much foundation. Fontana, one of Chopin's most intimate friends, denied its truth; Karasowski indignantly repudiates the idea. Chopin's education cannot have been very costly; and it would certainly have been surprising if his father, a professor at three large academies and the proprietor of a flourishing boarding school, had found it necessary to accept the charity of an outsider, however distinguished. Chopin, of course, could not go travelling for nothing, and he had expensive tastes. Substantial presents may have been made to him by Prince Radziwill. Such things were frequently done, and no one's dignity was hurt. But the gift of 'a good and complete education' is an entirely different matter; we may regard it as another of the many fictions of Chopin's biographers.

The young musician passed his final examination at the Lyceum in 1827. At this examination he did not make any great mark, and for a very good reason. He was now devoting himself more and more to music, less and less to general study. He had by this time composed his Variations for piano and orchestra on *Là ci darem* from Mozart's *Don Giovanni* (Op. 2); the first Sonata, in C minor (Op. 4), and the *Rondo à là Mazur* (Op. 5) were about to follow. The bent of his mind had been anxiously watched by his father for years, and the time appeared to have arrived for a decision in regard to his future. There does not seem to have been much hesitation about it. A practical, matter-of-fact parent would have made a fuss over his son risking the uncertainties of a musical career. But Nicholas Chopin had himself a good deal of the artistic temperament. He recognized that it would be foolish to thwart the evident direction of Frederic's genius; and so it was finally resolved that his son should be allowed to devote himself to the art of which he was soon to become so remarkable an exponent.

CHAPTER II

BERLIN AND VIENNA

HAVING thus decided about his son's future, Nicholas Chopin began to realize that some acquaintance with the outer world would be advisable as a preliminary to settling down to the practice of his profession. Warsaw was a small place after all—isolated, moreover, from the great centres of artistic and intellectual life—and could hardly be expected to satisfy the longings of a young genius to hear the masterpieces of the classic composers performed by the best artists. After another summer holiday at Strzyzewo, he was to visit one of these centres. The question was whether it should be Vienna or Berlin.

Chance led to a decision in favour of Berlin. Dr. Jarocki, the professor of zoology at the university, an intimate friend of Nicholas Chopin, had been invited to attend a scientific congress, presided over by Alexander von Humboldt, at Berlin, and, calling one day, he offered to take the young musician with him. Chopin was delighted. The congress was nothing to him: indeed he refused a ticket of admission to the meetings. What should he do among those bald heads? he asked. But the prospect of enlarging his musical experience in one of the leading European centres of his art was too tempting to be lost. 'It will give me,' he wrote, 'an opportunity of at any rate hearing a good opera once, and so having an idea of a perfect performance, which is worth a great deal of trouble.' He would meet all the best musicians, too—Mendelssohn, Zelter, Spontini[1] and others. The mere anticipation made him almost crazy, until on the day for starting he was 'writing like a lunatic, for I really do not know what I am about.'

The two travellers left Warsaw on 9th September 1828. It was the period of lumbering diligences and bottomless roads, and the journey to Berlin took five days. Rossini, like Ruskin, decried railways, which he described as a means of locomotion little suggestive of art and entirely at variance with nature. Chopin, by all accounts, would have been glad to dispense with the Rossini sentiment in favour of a tolerable measure of comfort. But he got to Berlin, and that was the main thing. By the middle of the month he was writing to his parents from the Hotel Kronprinz, where he had established himself. There are in existence three of his letters of this date which give his family a very vivid and often amusing account of how the young artist, plunged for the first time into the great world, occupied himself. As literary productions Chopin's letters disappoint even moderate expectations; but when they deal with his travels they at least serve to show that he was an intelligent and keen observer. The first letter from Berlin may be quoted in full. It is dated 16th September, and runs as follows:

My dearly beloved Parents and Sisters,

We arrived safely in this big, big city about three o'clock on Sunday afternoon, and went direct from the post to the hotel *Zum Kronprinz,* where we are now. It is a good and comfortable house.

---

[1] In the letter quoted in the next sentence Chopin says: 'I shall meet the most important musicians of Berlin, with the exception of Spontini.'—E. B.

Chopin

The very day we arrived Professor Jarocki took me to Lichtenstein's, where I met Humboldt. He is not above the middle height, and his features cannot be called handsome, but the prominent, broad brow, and the deep penetrating glance reveal the searching intellect of the scholar, who is as great a philanthropist as he is a traveller. He speaks French like his mother tongue; even you would have said so, dear father.

Lichtenstein promised to introduce me to the first musicians here and regretted that we had not arrived a few days sooner to have heard his daughter perform at a *matinée*, last Sunday, with orchestral accompaniments.

I, for my part, felt but little disappointment, but whether rightly or wrongly I know not, for I have neither seen nor heard the young lady. The day we arrived there was a performance of *The Interrupted Sacrifice*,[1] but our visit to Lichtenstein prevented me from being present.

Yesterday the savants [2] had a grand dinner; Humboldt did not occupy the chair, but a very different-looking person,[3] whose name I cannot at this moment recall. However, as he is, no doubt, some celebrity, I have written his name under my portrait of him. (I could not refrain from making some caricatures, which I have already docketed.) The dinner lasted so long that there was not time for me to hear Birnbach, the much-praised violinist of nine years. To-day I shall dine alone, having made my excuses to Jarocki, who readily perceived that, to a musician, the performance of such a work as Spontini's *Ferdinand Cortez* must be more interesting than an interminable dinner among philosophers. Now I am quite alone, and enjoying a chat with you, my dear ones.

There is a rumour that the great Paganini is coming here. I only hope it is true. Prince Radziwill is expected on the 20th of

---

[1] By Winter.

[2] 'All those learned caricatures,' according to E. L. Voynich's more vivid but less complete translation.—E. B.

[3] 'Some other Master of Spigots.'—E. L. Voynich.

this month. It will be a great pleasure to me if he comes. I have, as yet, seen nothing but the zoological collection, but I know the city pretty well, for I wandered among[1] the beautiful streets and bridges for two whole days. You shall have a verbal description of these, as also of the large and decidedly beautiful castle. The chief impression Berlin makes upon me is that of a straggling city which could, I think, contain double its present large population. We wanted to have stayed in the Französische Strasse, but I am very glad we did not, for it is as broad as our Leszno,[2] and needs ten times as many people as are in it to take off its desolate appearance.

To-day will be my first experience of the music of Berlin. Do not think me one-sided, dearest papa, for saying that I would much rather have spent the morning at Schlesinger's than in labouring through the thirteen rooms of the Zoological Museum, but I came here for the sake of my musical education, and Schlesinger's library, containing, as it does, the most important musical works of every age and country, is, of course, of more interest to me than any other collection. I console myself with the thought that I shall not miss Schlesinger's, and that a young man ought to see all he can, as there is something to be learnt everywhere. This morning I went to Kisling's pianoforte manufactory, at the end of the long Friedrichstrasse, but as there was not a single instrument completed, I had my long walk in vain. Fortunately for me there is a good grand piano in our hotel, which I play on every day, both to my own and the landlord's gratification.

The Prussian diligences are most uncomfortable, so the journey was less agreeable than I had anticipated; however, I reached the capital of the Hohenzollerns in good health and spirits. Our travelling companions were a German lawyer, living at Posen, who tried to distinguish himself by making coarse jokes, and a very fat farmer, with a smattering of politeness acquired by travelling.

At the last stage before Frankfort-on-Oder, a German Sappho

---

[1] 'Poked about and gaped at.'—Ibid.

[2] A long, wide street in Warsaw.

entered the diligence and poured forth a torrent of ridiculous, egotistical complaints.[1] Quite unwittingly, the good lady amused me immensely, for it was as good as a comedy when she began to argue with the lawyer, who, instead of laughing at her, seriously controverted everything she said.

The suburbs of Berlin, on the side by which we approached, are not pretty, but the scrupulous cleanliness and order which everywhere prevail are very pleasing to the eye. To-morrow I may visit the suburbs on the other side.

The congress will commence its sittings the day after to-morrow, and Lichtenstein has promised me a ticket. In the evening Alex. von Humboldt will receive the members at his house: Professor Jarocki offered to procure me an invitation, but I thanked him and said I should gain little, if any, intellectual advantage from such a gathering, for which I was not learned enough; besides, the professional gentlemen might cast questioning glances at a layman like me, and ask: 'Is Saul also among the prophets?' I fancied, even at the dinner, that my neighbour, Professor Lehmann, a celebrated botanist from Hamburg, looked at me rather curiously. I was astonished at the strength of his small fist; he broke with ease the large piece of white bread, to divide which I was fain to use both hands and a knife. He leaned over the table to talk to Jarocki, and in the excitement of the conversation missed his own plate and began to drum upon mine. A real *savant,* was he not? with that great ungainly nose, too. All this time I was on thorns, and as soon as he had finished with my plate, I wiped off the marks of his fingers with my napkin as fast as possible.

Marylski cannot have an atom of taste if he thinks the Berlin ladies dress well; their clothes are handsome, no doubt, but alas for the beautiful stuffs cut up for such puppets!—Your ever fondly loving

FREDERIC.

---

[1] 'Full of *achs* and *jas* and *nas*; in a word, a real romantic doll.'— E. L. Voynich.

The second letter, dated 20th September, is less interesting. It tells how, at the opera, he had heard Spontini's *Ferdinand Cortez,* Cimarosa's *Matrimonio segreto* and Onslow's *Colporteur.* These performances, he says, he greatly enjoyed; but he was 'quite carried away' by Handel's *Ode for St. Cecilia's Day* at the Singakademie. 'This,' he wrote, 'most nearly approaches my ideal of sublime music.' He had been to one of the congress meetings, and sat quite close to the crown prince. Spontini, Zelter and Mendelssohn were there, too, 'but I did not speak to any of them, as I did not think it proper to introduce myself.' Chopin's modesty again! He goes on to describe a visit to the Royal Library, 'which is very large but does not contain many musical works.' He saw, how-ever, an autograph letter of Kosciuszko's, and was 'much interested.'

One awkward incident he recounts with a comically feigned distress. At the Singakademie, observing a lady talking to 'a man in a kind of livery,' he asked his neighbour if that were a royal valet de chambre. 'That,' replied his neighbour, 'is His Excellency Baron von Humboldt.' 'You may imagine,' says Chopin, 'how very thankful I was that I had only uttered my question in a whisper; but I assure you that the Chamberlain's uniform changes even the countenance, or I could not have failed to recognize the great traveller who has ascended the mighty Chimborazo.' The physiognomies of the German savants struck the young Pole as rather odd, and he could not refrain from caricaturing 'these worthy but somewhat strange-looking gentlemen,' carefully adding the names, 'in case they should prove to be celebrities.' The letter closes with an expression of eager relish at the prospect of hearing Weber's *Freischütz,* which had been staged at Warsaw in 1826, but unfortunately the subsequent communication printed by Karasowski has nothing to say of the opera. Chopin was never really intensely interested in opera. It was not in his line.

The third letter, dated 27th September, deals chiefly with a 'grand dinner' given by the naturalists the day before the close of the congress. Functions of the kind are apt to prove a bore to most people, but Chopin found the dinner 'really very lively and entertaining.' The following extract is interesting and amusing:

Several very fair convivial songs were sung, in which all the company joined more or less heartily. Zelter conducted, and a large golden cup, standing on a red pedestal in front of him as a sign of his exalted musical merits, appeared to give him much satisfaction. The dishes were better that day than usual, they say, 'because the naturalists have been principally occupied during their sittings with the improvement of meats, sauces, soups, etc.' They make fun of these learned gentlemen in like manner at the König-stadt Theatre. In a play in which some beer is drunk, someone asks: 'Why is beer so good in Berlin now?' 'Why, because the naturalists are holding their conference,' is the answer.

After a stay of some fourteen days in Berlin the professor and the young musician set off on the return journey to Warsaw—a journey apparently more leisurely than pleasant. Mrs. Carlyle once celebrated a fellow-passenger as having 'the highest of all terrestrial qualities' because he was silent. Chopin's fellow-passengers were far from being silent. In the diligence were two gentlemen who talked eternally about politics, and talk about politics was as little agreeable to Chopin as it was to Shelley. Moreover, the two gentlemen smoked incessantly. Chopin disliked smoking. One of the travellers announced that he was going to smoke until he went to sleep, and would rather die than give up his pipe. This was too much for the musician, who, determined to have fresh air at any risk, went outside.

The travellers were to break their journey at Posen by invitation of the Archbishop Wolicki, but midway between that town and Frankfort-on-Oder they halted at a small village called Züllichau. There a singular incident happened while they were waiting to have the horses changed. It is Karasowski who tells the story. The professor had gone to see about his dinner; Chopin, thinking of less material things, wandered into one of the rooms at the inn, and there found a grand piano. The instrument did not look promising—the innkeeper's piano seldom does—but appearances are proverbially deceptive. Chopin rattled off a few arpeggios and then exclaimed in delighted surprise: 'O Sancta Cecilia, the piano is in tune!' The sensation can readily be imagined: sitting for days in a diligence and then having a good piano to play on! Chopin began to improvise *con amore*. One traveller after another came and stood round the instrument; the postmaster and his buxom wife followed; the servants brought up the rear. It reminds one of Burns's arrival at the wayside hostelries, when ostlers and everybody else within call gathered to hear him talk. Chopin became oblivious to everything and played on as he had played at that church service when the priest made a sudden end of his ecstasy. At last, when every one was listening in rapt attention to 'the elegant arabesques' sparkling from the musician's fingers, a stentorian voice called out: 'Gentlemen, the horses are ready.' The listeners looked as if they could strangle the man. 'Confound the disturber!' roared the innkeeper, and the whole company echoed him.

Chopin rose from the instrument, but was implored to go on. 'Stay and play, noble young artist,' cried Boniface.

'I will give you couriers' horses if you will only remain a little longer.' 'Do be persuaded,' insinuated Madame Boniface, who threatened the hesitating player with an embrace. What could Chopin do but resume his improvisation? When he had exhausted himself they brought him wine and cakes, and the women 'filled the pockets of the carriage with the best eatables that the house contained.' One of the company, an old man, went up to Chopin, and, 'in a voice trembling with emotion,' exclaimed: 'I, too, play the piano, and so know how to appreciate your masterly performance: if Mozart had heard it he would have grasped your hand and cried "Bravo!"' Finally, the landlord seized the musician in his arms and carried him to the conveyance, the postilion growling the while that 'the like of us must climb laboriously on to the box by ourselves.'

Long after, if we may credit the too credulous Karasowski, Chopin would recall this episode with sincere pleasure, assuring his friends that the highest praise lavished on him by the press had never given him so much satisfaction as the naïve homage of the German at the inn, who, in his eagerness to hear, let his pipe go out.[1] It is a very pretty story altogether, but one feels more than sceptical about the embellishments.

---

[1] It is told of Mendelssohn that, just after he had been presented by the King of Prussia with the Order of Merit, he and a friend were walking at Frankfort, when they came to a bridge. The friend waited to pay toll, while Mendelssohn walked on. 'That little gentleman,' said the toll-keeper—'is that the Mr. Mendelssohn who writes the partsongs that we sing in our choral society?' He was answered in the affirmative. 'Then, if you please, I should like to pay the toll for him myself.' Mendelssohn was greatly delighted. 'H'm,' said he, 'I like that much better than the Order.' The one anecdote recalls the other.

Chopin may, indeed, have amused himself for half an hour with the Züllichau piano, but it was not in his nature to enact the part of showman before a miscellaneous crowd of travellers, and innkeepers and domestics.

After spending a short time with the Archbishop of Posen, the professor and his companion took the road for Warsaw, and on 6th October Chopin was again in the bosom of his family. The year 1829 was notable to him from the fact that he then made the acquaintance of Hummel, who stayed for some time in Warsaw, giving concerts there. No record has survived of the interview between the two artists, but we are assured that they 'made a good impression on each other, and that their subsequent intercourse bears witness to much cordiality on the elder's side, and to an unquestioning and unbroken hero-worship on the younger's.' Hummel was one of a trio of pianoforte virtuosi of his period, the two others being Moscheles and Kalkbrenner. Berlioz described him as 'a man of great talent, a severe pianist.' He had been a pupil of Mozart, and was for some time Beethoven's rival in love, having married a sister of the singer Roeckel to whom Beethoven was much attached. A musician of this calibre could hardly fail to interest the young Pole, whose style as a composer, if it was influenced by anybody, probably owed more to Hummel than to any other contemporary artist.[1]

In this year, too, Chopin had the pleasure of hearing Paganini. The wizard violinist naturally appealed to him mainly in the character of a phenomenon, but that he admired him to a certain extent is indicated by the *Souvenir de Paganini*, which is supposed to belong to this period. This composition, said to be in the key of A major, was first published in the

[1] With the exception of Bellini and Field, who influenced him in melody and form respectively; but that came later.—E. B.

supplement of the Warsaw *Echo Muzyczne*. It is so rare that Niecks had never seen a copy when he wrote his life of Chopin. Paderewski, however, told Huneker that he possessed the piece, and that it was decidedly weak, 'having historic interest only.'

It is not improbable, as Sir Henry Hadow suggests, that these visits of Hummel and Paganini excited in Chopin the desire for a more extended artistic life than could be found in Warsaw. There he had been judged, and judged leniently, by kind-hearted compatriots; why should he not have his measure taken in a larger arena and by those who had no preliminary prejudice in his favour? Berlin he had already tried: supposing he should now try Vienna. He had, some time before this, sent certain of his manuscripts to Haslinger, and as he had received no tidings of their fate, why not, he argued, beard the publisher in his den?

In July, therefore, we find him setting out for the Austrian capital accompanied by his friends Maciejowski, Hube and Celinski—the first, a nephew of the famous writer on Slavonic law. The party halted for a week at Cracow, the ancient capital of the Poles, and continuing the journey by Ojcow, the so-called Polish Switzerland, they reached Vienna on 31st July. In his first letter home Chopin describes his journey in some detail, telling how he enjoyed to perfection the picturesque scenery of Galicia, Upper Silesia and Moravia, and giving an account of an adventure involving a drenching that must have been highly dangerous to one of his constitution. The second letter, dated 8th August, deals with matters almost strictly musical. He writes:

I am well and in good spirits. Why, I do not know, but the people here are astonished at me, and I wonder at them for finding anything to wonder at in me. I am indebted to good Elsner's letter of recommendation for my exceedingly friendly reception by Haslinger. He did not know how to make me sufficiently welcome; he showed me all the musical novelties he had, made his son play to me, and apologized for not introducing his wife, who had just gone out. In spite of all his politeness, he has not yet printed my compositions. I did not ask him about them, but he said, when showing me one of his finest editions, that my Variations on *Là ci darem la mano* were to appear next week, in the same style, in *Odeon*. This I certainly had not expected. He strongly advised me to play in public, although it is summer and therefore not a favourable time for concerts.

This suggestion that he should play in public appears to have somewhat surprised the modest young artist. To play in Warsaw was all very well, but to play 'in a city which can boast of having heard a Haydn, a Mozart and a Beethoven,' that was a distinction he had not dreamed of achieving just yet. Musical Vienna, to its credit, set itself very warmly to overcome his diffidence. 'Wherever I show myself,' writes Chopin, 'I am besieged with requests to play.' *Capellmeister* Würfel insisted that, as his compositions were about to appear, he must give a concert, otherwise he would have to return to Vienna for the purpose. 'If you have composed anything new,' said he, 'and want it to create a sensation, you must play it yourself.' Blahetka, a prominent journalist whom he met at Haslinger's, was of the same mind. 'Blahetka thinks I shall make a furore,' he writes, 'for, as he puts it, I am "an artist of the first rank and worthy to be placed beside Moscheles, Herz and Kalkbrenner."' Stein said he would send one of his instruments for use at the proposed concert; Graff, whose pianos Chopin preferred, offered a like favour. And so, unable to resist the appeals of so many disinterested friends, Chopin agreed to give the concert. Würfel prepared the bills and advertisements; Count Gallenberg, now the husband of Giulietta Ciicciardi, who as a young girl have been loved by Beethoven, lent the Kärnthnerthor Theatre, and on 11th August the young player made his first appearance before the critical Viennese public. The programme included Beethoven's Overture to *Prometheus,* the *Don Giovanni* Variations, the *Krakowiak Rondo*,[1] an aria of Rossini's and one of Vaccai's, sung by Mlle Veltheim, a celebrated bravura vocalist. The best extant accounts of the recital are from the player's own pen. Writing to his friend Woyciechowski,[2] Chopin says:

This first appearance before the Viennese public did not in the least excite me, and I sat down to play on a splendid instrument of Graff's, perhaps the best in Vienna. A painted young man, who prided himself upon having performed the same service for Moscheles, Hummel and Herz, turned over the leaves for me in the Variations. Notwithstanding that I was in a desperate mood the Variations pleased so much that I was recalled several times. Mlle Veltheim sang exquisitely, and my improvisation was followed by much applause and many recalls.

In a letter to his parents he tells that his Warsaw friends distributed themselves among the audience, 'that they might hear the observations of the critics and the various opinions of the public.' Celinski heard nothing unfavourable; Hube

[1] This was not played, however. According to a letter Chopin wrote home the next day, it went so badly at rehearsal that he decided to substitute an improvisation. He chose for his themes a melody from Boieldieu's *Dame blanche* and a Polish drinking song, *Chmiel.—*E. B.

[2] Titus Woyciechowski now lived on his family estate in Poland. The bulk of Chopin's letters, apart from those written to his parents, are addressed to him. Several are also addressed to Jan Matuzynski, who studied medicine at Warsaw and later joined Chopin in Paris.

reported 'the most severe criticism.' He had overheard a lady remark: 'A pity the youth has so little presence.' No doubt, as Sir Henry Hadow observes, like the wife of Charles Lamb's friend, she had expected to see a 'tall, fine, officer-looking man,' who would look well in uniform. The audience, as a whole, was cordial and appreciative, rising indeed to enthusiasm when Chopin began to improvise on the song sung by the Poles at marriage ceremonies while the bride's sisters place the cap on her head. At that point, according to Chopin's 'spies in the pit,' the people began a regular dance on the benches. The only adverse criticism is frankly noticed by Chopin himself. 'There is,' he writes, 'an almost unanimous opinion that I play too softly, or rather too delicately, for the public here—that is to say, they are accustomed to the drum-beating of their own piano virtuosi. I am afraid the newspapers will say the same thing, especially as the daughter of one of the editors drums dreadfully; but never mind if it be so: I would much rather they said I played too gently than too roughly.' Even in this matter he had the consolation of having especially pleased the nobility. 'The Schwarzenbergs and Wobrzes and others were quite enthusiastic about the delicacy and elegance of my execution,' he says. 'My manner of playing pleases the ladies so much.'

What the newspapers said is of no great account now, for, as Schumann observed, 'one bar of Chopin is worth more than a whole year of musical criticism.' But Chopin was stupidly sensitive. Thus he wrote: 'If the newspapers cut me up so much that I shall not venture before the world again I have resolved to become a house-painter. That would be as easy as anything else, and I should at any rate still be an artist.' Later he learned to accept ill-natured criticism more placidly. For the present, luckily, the newspapers did not cut him up. On the contrary, they praised him very highly; and altogether the result of this first experiment in concert-giving was that he found himself 'at least four years wiser and much more experienced.'

Thus encouraged by press and public, Chopin arranged to give a second recital on 18th August. As he played gratui-tously on both occasions it is clear that he was in no stress of poverty, as some of his biographers would have us believe. Indeed, he writes on 19th August that his finances are 'still in the best order.' Under no circumstances, he continues, would he give a third concert. 'I only give a second because I am forced to, and I thought that people might say in Warsaw: "He only gave *one* concert in Vienna, so he could not have been much liked."' The audience at this second concert was larger than on the former occasion, and the applause still more encouraging. Even when he came on the stage he was greeted with 'three long rounds of applause.' Writing the following day, he says:

The profession praise my Rondo,[1] one and all, from *Capellmeister* Lachner to the piano-tuner. I know I have pleased the ladies and the musicians. Gyrowetz, who sat next Celinski, called *Bravo!* and made a tremendous noise. The only people not satisfied were the out-and-out Germans.[2] Yesterday one of them, who had just come from the theatre, sat down to eat at the table I was sitting at. His acquaintance asked him how he liked the performance. 'The ballet is pretty,' was his answer. 'But the concert, what of that?' they asked. Instead of replying he began to talk of something

---

[1] The *Krakowiak Rondo* was played this time, at the request of the stage manager of the Kärnthnerthor Theatre, who had liked it greatly at the rehearsal for the first concert.—E. B.

[2] E. L. Voynich translates: 'I only don't know whether I pleased the stony Germans.'

else, from which I conclude that he recognized me, although my back was towards him. I felt bound to relieve him from the restraint of my presence and went to bed saying to myself: 'The man has not been born yet who does everything right.' . . . Schuppanzigh said yesterday that as I was leaving Vienna so quickly, I must come again soon. I answered that I should gladly return for the sake of further improving myself, to which the baron replied that for such a reason I should never need to come, for I had nothing more to learn. This opinion was confirmed by the others. These are indeed mere compliments, but one does not listen to them unwillingly. For the future I shall at any rate not be regarded as a student.

The newspaper notices were all that Chopin could desire. The leading organ of musical criticism at that time was the *Wiener Theaterzeitung*, which every artist used to dread as much as authors dreaded the old slashing *Saturday Review*. It said:

He plays very quietly, with little emphasis, and with none of that rhetorical aplomb which is considered indispensable by virtuosi. . . . He was recognized as an artist of whom the best may be expected as soon as he has heard more music. . . . He knows how to please, although in his case the desire to make good music predominates noticeably over the desire to give pleasure.

This view of the player's powers was taken for the most part by all the minor journals, and the whole city 'swelled its voice into a full chorus of approval.' As Sir Henry Hadow says, even the distant *Allgemeine musikalische Zeitung* caught an echo of the enthusiasm and hailed Chopin as a 'brilliant meteor' who had appeared on the 'horizon without any previous blast of trumpets.'

Chopin came away from Vienna delighted with his visit. The city, he said, is 'handsome, lively, and pleases me exceedingly.' When he got home he wrote to Woyciechowski that it had 'utterly stupefied and infatuated' him. He made the acquaintance of many musical people too: Gyrowetz, *Capell-meister* of the Court Opera (whose concerto he had played at his first concert in Warsaw); Franz Lachner, the friend of Schubert; Conradin Kreutzer; Seyfried, the composer and correspondent of the *Allgemeine musikalische Zeitung*; Mayseder, the leading Viennese violinist of the day, and many others. He became very intimate with Czerny, and often played duets for two pianos with him. 'He is a good-natured man but nothing more,' Chopin wrote. When the farewell came, 'Czerny was warmer than all his compositions.' Count Lichnowski, Beethoven's friend, with his wife and daughter, showed him 'a great deal too much kindness'; and Schup-panzigh, whose team was the first to play Beethoven's quartets and over whose corpulence the great man used to chuckle, paid him many compliments. In fact, he had, as he says, conquered 'the learned and those who have poetic tempera-ments.' He heard a good deal of music: Boieldieu's *Dame blanche,* Meyerbeer's *Crociato in Egitto* and other operas,[1] and on the whole enjoyed himself immensely.

From Vienna, which he left on 19th August, Chopin first went on to Prague, and then to Teplitz and Dresden. At Prague, where he stayed for 'three delightful days,' he met Pixis, professor of the violin at the Conservatoire; August Klengel,[2] a noted piano virtuoso and court organist at Dresden,

---

[1] In his letter of 8th August he says: 'To-day *Joseph in Egypt.*' E. L. Voynich asks in a footnote: 'Is this an error for Rossini's *Mosè in Egitto?*' But why not Méhul's *Joseph,* the German version of which is called *Joseph in Aegypten?*—E. B.

[2] Chopin had a letter of introduction to Klengel from Vienna and intended to look him up at Dresden, but found him staying with Pixis in Prague.—E. B.

who attempted to match Bach's *Well-tempered Clavier* with his canons and fugues in all major and minor keys; and other celebrities. In one of his letters he says he listened to Klengel's fugues for more than two hours—a somewhat trying ordeal one would imagine, especially for Chopin, who had no leanings towards the purely scientific in musical composition. 'Klengel's playing pleased me,' he writes, 'but to speak candidly, I had expected something better still.' Nevertheless, it was 'a very agreeable acquaintanceship, and I value it more highly than Czerny's.' He was pressed to give a recital at Prague, but declined, because he had no desire to risk forfeiting the renown he had won in Vienna. 'As even Paganini was sharply criticized, I shall take care not to perform in this place.' Already he was mindful of his reputation.

At Teplitz an evening was spent at Prince Clary's, where he improvised on a theme from Rossini's *Moses* and had to play four times in order to satisfy the company. The visit to Dresden, where he arrived in the evening of 26th August, was distinguished by a notable incident recounted by Wodzinski. A certain Madame Dobrzycka invited Chopin to spend an evening with her 'with a few friends.' He met what he called a small but respectable company: two ladies of venerable aspect and a man some thirty years old, with fine features and clean-shaven face, whom he took to be a savant or a parson. Chopin was introduced as a young compatriot, an artist of great talent, and asked to play. He was listened to in the deep silence he appreciated better than the most noisy applause. When he ended, what was his surprise to hear Madame Dobrzycka say, with tears in her eyes: 'Thanks; you have given a delightful treat to Her Majesty and their highnesses.' The ladies were the queen and Princess Augusta; the 'savant' was Prince John, a well-read man, translator of

Dante, and one day to be King of Saxony. This visit to Dresden happened very opportunely, for Goethe's eightieth birthday was being celebrated, and the first part of *Faust*, with fragments from Spohr's opera of the same name doing service for incidental music, was performed in Dresden for the first time. 'A fearful but magnificent conception' is Chopin's only comment. For the rest he saw 'the world-renowned gallery, the fruit show and the gardens,' paid some visits, made the aequaintance of Morlacchi, musical director to the court, whom Wagner succeeded as a conductor in 1843, and then hurried home, reaching Warsaw on 12th September 1829.

Thus ended what may be called Chopin's *Wanderjahre*. He had experienced something which might be taken as counter-acting the cosseting and the adulation of his home life. Hitherto he had led, as it were, a parochial existence; he had now seen something of a gayer, a freer and an infinitely more artistic life. Wider views, riper judgment and a better knowledge of human nature were the result. Warsaw could no longer be a home for him. The severance was not to come just yet, but it could not be delayed much longer.

CHAPTER III

LOVE AFFAIRS

BACK in Warsaw among his own people, among his own familiar friends, after the triumphs of Vienna, Chopin might have been perfectly happy. Unfortunately he fell in love and was miserable. This was the first of several love affairs we shall have to consider. George Sand, who could speak from experience, remarked upon his 'emotional versatility' in the matter of losing his heart—temporarily. He could, it was said, fall in and out of love in an evening; a crumpled rose-leaf was sufficient cause to induce frowns and capricious flights. It was not quite as bad as that. Chopin never lost his wits over any woman except in his letters. But un-doubtedly, like Laurence Sterne, he did find that it 'harmonized the soul' to have some Dulcinea always in his head. We may try to explain it in various ways. A French philosopher, Paul Janet, says that nobody ever falls in love unless, in the common slang, he is a bit 'off colour.' Dr. Johnson says it is usually the weak individual who falls in love. These are mere witticisms. Chopin fell in love, as the average man does, because he could not help it. And I am Philistine enough to think that it was good for him that he did fall in love. Goethe's flirtations contributed something to his artistic development. Half of Burns's finest songs were inspired by individual beauties who had struck the poet's fancy; and if we could read close enough into Chopin's compositions I have no doubt we should see his loves mirrored there too.

Apparently there had been some little flirtation with Leopoldine Blahetka in Vienna, for Chopin writes of his regret at parting with that charming girl, who was still in her teens, and tells how she gave him as a souvenir a copy of her compositions. But this was a passing fancy. With Chopin 'out of sight, out of mind' was a proverb of precise application. The lady who now became the object of his devouring passion bore the name of Konstancja Gladkowska. She was a vocalist and a student at the Warsaw Conservatoire. Liszt describes her as 'sweet and beautiful.'

The first that we hear of the affair is in a letter to Woyciechowski. Remarking that in no case would he stay the winter in Warsaw, Chopin goes on to say: 'Do not think for one moment that, when I urge the advantage of a stay in Vienna, I am thinking of Miss Blahetka, of whom I have already written to you; for I have—perhaps to my misfortune—already found my ideal, which I worship faithfully and sincerely. Six months have now passed, and I have not yet exchanged a word with her of whom I nightly dream. Whilst thinking of her I composed the *adagio* of my Concerto, and early this morning she inspired the Waltz[1] which I send you with this letter.' A little later he writes: 'It is bitter to have no one with whom one can share joy or sorrow, to feel one's heart oppressed, and to be unable to express one's complaints to any human soul.'

One thinks of Hector Berlioz's mad passion for Harriet Smithson, the pretty Irish actress, who cost the composer many nights' sleep before he could summon up the courage to let her hear his voice. There was nothing but Chopin's

[1] The Concerto in F minor and the Waltz in D flat major, (Op. 70).

indecision and timidity to prevent him—a musician who had practically conquered Berlin and Vienna—from seeking an introduction to a pupil of the Warsaw Conservatoire. But this was just one of the Chopin characteristics. Chopin loved, but had not the courage to tell the beloved one. He put his passion on paper, he played it, but speak it he could not. Music was indeed to him the 'food of love.' One must not write dogmatically on such a theme. As the rustic in Thomas Hardy's novel remarks, the 'queerest things on earth belong to' the business of love-making. Men of much stronger grain have been just as timid as Chopin was in their dealings with the fair sex. But taking all the other characteristics into account, it cannot well be denied that the episode reveals in a very striking way his native indecision, his inability to make up his mind. He experienced something like an atrophy of the will, for he could neither proclaim his love nor fly from Warsaw, as he constantly declared he must do. Like many other men of genius, he suffered all his life from *folie de doute*.

That he was very seriously in love with Konstancja Gladkowska—for the time being—there is no reason to disbelieve. In one letter he says: 'God forbid that she should suffer in any way on my account. Let her mind be at rest, and tell her that so long as my heart beats I shall not cease to adore her. Tell her that, even after death, my ashes shall be strewn beneath her feet.' When she made her first appearance on the operatic stage he launched forth extravagantly in her praise; when he gave a concert and invited her to sing he became more enraptured than ever because she 'wore a white dress and roses in her hair, and was charmingly beautiful.' Her 'low B came out so magnificently that Zielinski declared it alone was worth a thousand ducats.' A man who could write like that was obviously 'to madness near allied.' Genius may indeed be, as some contend, a form of insanity. But then so many people who are not geniuses are insanely in love!

The course of this true love of Chopin's is very difficult to follow. I say 'true love' advisedly; for, although Chopin was notoriously fickle in his fancies, I cannot help feeling that fate would have done him a real service by giving him this evidently admirable girl for a wife. Konstancja Gladkowska's own destiny was unfortunate for Chopin, unfortunate for herself. Liszt gushes over the affair in the fashion peculiar to him, but he is probably not so far wrong as some have supposed. He says: 'The tempest, which in one of its sudden gusts tore Chopin from his native soil, like a dreamy and abstracted bird, surprised by the storm upon the branches of a foreign tree, sundered the ties of this first love and robbed the exile of a faithful and devoted wife, as well as disinherited him of a country.' More than one writer has made merry over the dreamy and abstracted bird upon a foreign tree; but in view of the later George Sand episode one sincerely wishes that Chopin had wooed and won Konstancja.

It is impossible to say how much of his restlessness in Warsaw was due to this passion and how much to a genuine longing for a larger artistic life, which his experiences in Vienna might well have engendered. What is certain is that Warsaw became hateful to him, and that he was perpetually forming projects for leaving it. He would go to Berlin, to Vienna, to Italy, to Paris—anywhere to get out of himself and enable him to forget the object of his idolatry. Yet this irresolute lover wavered, as he always did. He might never see Konstancja again. Perhaps he would die in the stranger's land, with the unconcerned physician at his bedside and the hired servants listening indifferently to his last breath.

A Vacillating Lover

Indecision was the keynote of the whole period. Plans were formed to-day to be reversed to-morrow, and every change was made 'the occasion for some fresh complaint or some new exhibition of a self-inflicted wound.' Never did lover torture himself so unnecessarily.

Perhaps, as Sir Henry Hadow thinks, it was not a genuine passion after all. It is not love which degrades a chivalrous nature, says that acute writer, which torments generosity with suspicions and turns activity into a feverish impatience. 'Grant that every lover has his moments of unreason, fits of groundless ill-temper, of disproportionate remorse, of jealousy that is roused by a look and quieted by a word, yet we are here bidden to mistake the accidents for the substance and to describe as love a shadow which is cast from no sun.' Hadow goes on to argue that Chopin's passion was not a cause but a symptom; not a power which influenced his life, but a direction of hectic energy that must itself be traced back to a remoter source.

Chopin was at the verge of manhood: always nervous and impressionable, he had come to the time when strength is weakest and courage most insecure. He had just passed through the bewilderment of his first great enterprise and had emerged to breathe an atmosphere electric with change and heavy with disquietude. 'It is little wonder that he lost his true self and strayed from his appointed course. He would have been more than human if he had not felt some stress of uncertainty, or followed his restless impulses in the absence of a surer guide.'

There is something in this view, no doubt. The average self-reliant lover would have gone straight to his mistress and whispered in her ear alone the tale of his passion. Chopin sought relief from his friends. What he should have been

writing to Konstancja he wrote to Woyciechowski. 'You
have no idea how much I love you,' he told the latter. 'What
would I not give to embrace you once again?' And all the
time he was shrinking from laying open his heart to the one
who, for all that he knew, was ready to take him to her arms.

To leave this matter for a moment, however, it must not
be supposed that the period we are now considering was
devoid of other interests for Chopin. His father, worried by
his peevish plaints about a change of scene, suggested that he
should go to Berlin, where Prince Radziwill and his wife
wished to attach him to their household for a time. He did
not go to Berlin, but in October 1829 paid an eight days'
visit to the prince at Antonin. The prince, as we have already
learned, played the cello, and one of the daughters, as we now
gather, was an excellent pianist. There was thus some good
music-making together during the week of Chopin's stay,
and even a hint of solace for the distracted lover. In a letter
from Antonin, Chopin says: 'I have written during my stay
here an *Alla Polacca*,[1] with violoncello. It is nothing more
than a brilliant *salon* piece, such as pleases ladies. I should
like the Princess Wanda to practise it. She is only seventeen
years of age, and very beautiful; it would be delightful to have
the pleasure of placing her pretty fingers upon the keys.'
Chopin could hardly have aspired to the princess, though he
said of her mother: 'She knows quite well that the value of
a man does not depend on his descent.' Yet, for all that we
can tell, she may have given him some encouragement. He
subsequently announces that 'she has two portraits of me in
her album,' which in ordinary cases of the kind would usually
mean something.

[1] Introduction and Polonaise (Op. 3).

The winter of 1829–30—his last winter in his native town
—Chopin spent quietly at home in Warsaw, occupied with
the completion of the Concerto in F minor (Op. 21).[1] In
March two concerts were given, his first public appearances
on his own account in Warsaw. He cleared about £125,
a sum which the modern virtuoso would regard as small
enough, but which in those days was thought considerable.
At the first concert, on the 17th, the programme included the
F minor Concerto, the overture to one of Elsner's operas,
some variations by Paer, sung by Madame Meier, and a
potpourri on Polish airs. The old complaint was again
revived that Chopin did not play loud enough. Warsaw
desired the drum as much as Vienna. Edouard Wolff
declared to Niecks that in Warsaw they had no idea of the
real greatness of Chopin, which is only to repeat that the
prophet is without honour in his own country. But Chopin
was getting a little tired of hearing about the delicacy of his
tone. For once he would try to please the Warsaw public.
Accordingly, for the second concert, given on the 24th, he
sent to Vienna for one of Graff's pianos, [on which he not
only repeated the Concerto, but played the *Krakowiak Rondo*
and an improvisation.] The result was encouraging: press
and public acknowledged themselves satisfied. He seems,
indeed, to have created something like a furore. Congratula-
tions reached him from all sides. The Warsaw *Courier*
printed a sonnet in his honour; champagne was offered him
by a pianist named Dunst; and Orlowski 'dished up the
themes of his concerto into mazurkas, and had the impudence
to publish them.' One music seller asked for his portrait,
but was refused on the ground that he did not want to see his

[1] The first written by him; it was marked No. 2 because it was
published after the E minor Concerto.

face on cheese and butter wrappers. In fact, the whole thing was overdone, as Chopin thought. 'I will no longer read what people write about me,' he said in a petulant mood. Of course, he did not mean it. If he had lived to-day, he would have subscribed to a press-cutting agency.

One would imagine that in Warsaw the arts, and especially music, must have received but scant attention about the date at which we have now arrived. Poland was once more in a state of ferment. Alexander I had given the Poles a constitution, including biennial Diets, a responsible ministry, a separate army and liberty of the press. For some time matters seemed to go on smoothly, but a spirit of discontent had now developed. The 'great wave rolling eastward from Paris' did not break on Warsaw until November, but the clouds were already dark in the early summer, and a 'murmur of expectation' was in the air. The Diet met after an inter-regnum of five years, and the national discontent over Russia's administration found expression in fiery debate. Secret societies were formed; the nobles were busy with political intrigue; war became inevitable.

But all this was going on without, so far as we can see, much attention from Chopin. [He was busy in the spring and summer with the E minor Concerto (Op. 11)] and outside professional interests occasionally engaged him when certain notable artists presented themselves in Warsaw. He heard Henriette Sontag and wrote enthusiastically of her singing. Lipinski, the violinist, excited his admiration, and Mlle de Belleville, the pianist, pleased him as much as she pleased Schumann. He was generous in his appreciation of all fellow-artists, with exceptions in the case of composers, and when he found it necessary to say something uncomplimentary he generally begged that the remark might not be repeated.

Meanwhile the Gladkowska affair, with its unbearable longing, continued to tug at his heart-strings. The summer had gone, the winter was approaching, and he was still the victim of his undeclared passion. The old irresolution returned upon him. Konstancja had just made her first stage appearance in the title part of Paer's *Agnese*, and the event produced a fresh agitation. On 18th September he writes to Woyciechowski:

I have no special attraction anywhere, but, in any event, I shall not remain in Warsaw. If you think that it is some beloved object that keeps me here, you are wrong, like a good many other people. I can assure you that so far as I myself am concerned I am ready for any sacrifice. I love,[1] but I must keep my unhappy passion locked in my own breast for some years longer. . . . I was at great big Cichocki's yesterday, for his name-day, when I took part in Spohr's Quintet for piano, clarinet, bassoon, horn and flute. The work is extremely beautiful, but I do not find the pianoforte part very playable.[2] . . . Instead of commencing at seven o'clock we did not begin until eleven. You are doubtless surprised that I was not fast asleep. But there was a very good reason why I should keep awake, for among the guests was a very beautiful girl, who vividly reminded me of my ideal. Just fancy! I stayed till three a.m. . . . I intended to have started for Vienna this day week, but finally gave up the idea—perhaps you can guess why.

Of course, he gave up the idea because he could not tear himself away from the charmer. Perhaps he even thought of consoling himself by a flirtation with the pretty young lady who reminded him so vividly of his ideal. He was so hopelessly infatuated! It gave him the most exquisite delight to dine with a certain lady because she also bore 'the inexpressibly

---

[1] E. L. Voynich has: 'If I were in love . . .'
[2] 'Dreadfully unpianistic.'—Ibid.

dear name' of Konstancja. Nay, it set his heart in a flutter
to catch a glimpse of the 'dear name' embroidered on the
lady's handkerchiefs.

And Konstancja, what was her position in the matter all
this time? We do not know. It is certain that she saw very
little of Chopin. From his own letters we make out that for
a whole year he never once visited her. He worshipped at
a distance. We are in the dark, too, as to whether Konstancja
responded to his affection; it is not even certain that she was
aware of it. True, she gave him a ring—'my precious ring'
he called it—on his departure from Warsaw, but the positive
significance of the gift is nowhere indicated. The ring, as
Sir Henry Hadow says, should have been the beginning of a
more intimate romance, but, instead of that, it was virtually
the end of the story. It may have been another case of 'out
of sight, out of mind.'

After the composer left Warsaw he appears at any rate to
have had no further direct communication with Konstancja;
presently her name vanishes from his letters; and when she
marries a year later he takes the news with a momentary burst
of anger, and then dismisses the subject from his thoughts.
Some writers have blamed the lady for what they call her
'heartless treatment' of Chopin, but there is no ground for
any accusation of the kind. The whole episode is wrapped
in an impenetrable mystery.

We cannot tell whether Chopin declared his love. There
is nothing to show that he was a rejected suitor. The lady
married a Warsaw merchant in 1832—Wodzinski says she
subsequently became blind—but it is possible enough that
there was no attachment between her and her future husband
up to the time that Chopin left his home. It is unprofitable
in any case to dwell further on the matter. As James Huneker

says, if Konstancja was fickle, Chopin was inconstant, so 'let us waste no pity on the episode, over which lakes of tears have been shed and rivers of ink have been spilt.' The regrettable thing is that it should have affected Chopin's health. Heller, who saw him in Warsaw in 1830, described him to Niecks as thin and sunken, and added that already the people of Warsaw had marked him out for an early death.

Chopin gave his last concert in Warsaw on 11th October 1830. The leading item in the programme was the E minor Concerto, which he had completed in August, and which he now played piecemeal, the first and the last two movements being separated by an aria. [It was sung by a young vocalist named Wolkow, but Konstancja Gladkowska sang in the second part of the programme, to which Chopin contributed one of his improvisations.] The F minor Concerto had been treated in the same manner at the concert in March, the *allegro* being played as a separate piece, and the *adagio* and rondo following later. It was the custom of the time: audiences were not yet prepared to swallow an entire concerto at once, any more than the audiences of Handel's day were prepared to swallow *Israel in Egypt* without its being 'intermixed with songs.' Even in Paris Berlioz served out Beethoven's symphonies in sections.

Chopin played splendidly at this October concert. He said so himself, and he always knew better than his hearers when he did well or not well. He had to respond to four recalls. 'I believe I did it yesterday with a certain grace,' he writes, 'for Brandt had taught me how to do it properly.' This naïve remark refers to his platform bow. It reveals a certain mixture of innocent vanity and girlishness which was characteristic of Chopin. Pretty lace collars and deportment

—these were to him things of 'good report,' upon which he loved to dwell.

On 1st November Chopin left Warsaw, never to return. It was surely a mournful stroke of destiny which decided that he should not once see his country again. In the previous September he had written: 'I am convinced that I shall say farewell to my home for ever.' Strange presentiment. 'I am going out into the wide world,' he wrote now, as, with 'hopes and light regrets' in his heart, he took his last look of the towers of Warsaw. Nothing is said about the parting with his parents, but we may be sure that it was heartrending. His father he saw once more; his mother never again. At Wola, the first village beyond Warsaw, a romantic incident occurred. Elsner and the pupils of the Conservatoire met him, offered him a banquet, sang a cantata composed for the occasion by his old master, and presented him with a silver goblet filled with Polish earth. That same earth was, only a few years later, to be strewn on his coffin in distant Père Lachaise.

CHAPTER IV

INTO THE WIDE WORLD

CHOPIN was now no longer a temporary wanderer from the paternal roof: he had practically severed himself from his youth and had gone forth 'with the keyboard and a brain full of beautiful music as his only weapons.' Like the knights-errant of the old days of chivalry, he had only the vaguest notion of his ultimate destination. It was to be Vienna first —that much was certain; but whither the knight-errant was to proceed after Vienna—that was by no means certain. He might go to Berlin; he might go to Italy. Perhaps he would make for Paris; perhaps for London. Meanwhile he was on the road—now heavy of heart at having parted with parents and 'ideal'; again merry as a marriage-bell at the prospect of making a still more extended acquaintance with the great art world, of which as yet he could boast only a very limited experience.

It took him four weeks to reach Vienna, the journey being broken at several places on the way. At Kalisz he was joined by Woyciechowski, and the two proceeded to Breslau on 6th November. There Chopin made the acquaintance of Adolph Friedrich Hesse, a name once greatly revered by the older school of organists. Hesse, who is described by Chopin as 'the second local connoisseur,' played duets with him and paid him compliments which he was proud to acknowledge. At Breslau also he took the place of a timid amateur at a concert directed by his old friend *Capellmeister* Schnabel, and considerably astonished the audience by his rendering of the E minor Concerto. The good folk of Breslau did not know what to make of him. Chopin says that one discerning amateur praised the novelty of the form in the Concerto, and ingenuously adds that this was the man who understood him best. Schnabel, he writes, 'claps me on the shoulder every moment,' and his face 'beams with real delight.' But then, as a set-off to this, somebody was heard to remark that while the young man could certainly play, just as certainly he could not compose. For once Chopin got some amusement out of criticism. But what did it matter about Breslau after all?

The next halting-place of the travellers, on 12th November, was Dresden, where Chopin renewed his acquaintance with 'my dear Klengel,' and made several new friends. The famous gallery always formed an attraction. 'If I lived here,' he said, 'I would go to the gallery every week, for there are pictures there at the sight of which I imagine music.' At this time the thought of visiting Italy seems to have been uppermost in his mind (what inspiring pictures he would have found there!); and Rubini, a brother of the great tenor, as well as the 'incomparable Rolla,' the violinist, furnished him with letters of introduction which, as it turned out, he never had occasion to use. At an evening party at Dr. Kreissig's he was greatly tickled by the sight of a number of dames armed with knitting needles, which 'moved ceaselessly' during the intervals of the music; and getting into a sedan-chair for the first time, a spirit of mischief almost impelled him to kick out the bottom of the 'queer comfortable box.' He heard Auber's *La Muette de Portici* and Rossini's *Tancredi* at the opera, an indifferent Mass by a local nobleman at the court chapel, and was delighted with the cello performances of Dotzauer and Kummer. The cello was an instrument for which he had a 'consuming affection.' One wonders that he did not write more for it.

But Chopin declined to linger in Dresden. 'I don't think Dresden would bring me either much fame or much money, and I have no time to spare,' he said. Passing next through Prague, he reached Vienna at the end of November. With his former successes in the Austrian capital still fresh in his mind, he imagined that he had only to announce himself in order to have the musical public at his feet. He was speedily undeceived. The Viennese musical public had all but forgotten him. Those were not the days of interviews and photographs in the illustrated papers, with disquisitions on the virtuoso's slippers and cigarette smoking; and Chopin, so far, was not 'interesting' in the modern sense. It is said —Tarnowski is the authority—that he was always so particular about his dress and general appearance because he was irritated at the common artist's claim to genius on the strength of long hair and careless apparel and a sort of Manfred gloom that was supposed to go well with cloaks and Byron collars. One sympathizes with him; but it is just conceivable that if he had been a Pole with a chrysanthemum head he would not have vanished so completely from the Viennese memory. Yet the cause of Vienna's forgetfulness did not lie entirely with Chopin himself. Other artists had been heard in the meantime; and audiences, surfeited with classical music, professed themselves pleased with prosy conductors' compositions and the lighter fare of Johann Strauss and Lanner. The situation is very well indicated by Chopin's remark that 'waltzes are here called *works,* and almost nothing but waltzes are published.' That being so, we can easily understand that Haslinger would receive Chopin rather coldly, now that he was better acquainted with his compositions. The publisher had been almost embarrassingly enthusiastic on the occasion of the former visit; this time he was more cautious. He told Chopin that he could not possibly print the *Là ci darem* Variations, the manuscript of which had long been in his hands, and he sternly declined to have anything to do with the F minor Concerto, though Würfel had given his solemn assurance that it was better than Hummel's in A flat major.

It is easy to censure Haslinger now, to say that he was pig-headed, wanting in discernment, and so forth. But it is only in the rarest cases that the publisher can afford to play the philanthropist to young genius. His business is—as he must perforce conceive it—to get hold of marketable stuff; and it must be remembered that in 1831 the style of music which the public demanded was not Chopin's style. It was the public, not the publisher, who was to blame. Still, one regrets that Chopin should have met with this rebuff on the verge of his entry into the world. It probably helped to embitter him for the future, and it certainly depressed him for the moment.

Nor was it by any means the only disillusion he suffered in Vienna. Everything seemed to be out of joint. His old friends the Blahetkas had gone to Stuttgart; Würfel was not available; Schuppanzigh was ill. Count Gallenberg had lost heavily at the Kärnthnerthor Theatre and had retired in favour of a new manager, Louis Duport, formerly a dancer. To the latter Chopin was introduced by Hummel, but Duport 'would guarantee nothing, and did not encourage him to give a concert at all.' In short, as Chopin himself wrote in a letter to Elsner, 'I meet with obstacles on every hand. Not only does a series of wretched pianoforte concerts entirely ruin all real music and tire the public, but the occurrences in Poland have also had their effect upon my position.'

These occurrences were disturbing enough. Warsaw had now risen in revolt against the Russians: Woyciechowski rushed off from Vienna to join the insurgents; Chopin, disgusted with his reception and his prospects, and feeling acutely the loss of his friend, decided to do likewise, prompted more especially by anxiety about the safety of his parents. Happily, his usual vacillation prevented him from making a fool of himself—perhaps making himself the target of some Russian, to the eternal loss of music. It has been hinted that Chopin was a coward. He was nothing of the kind: he was 'psychically brave,' but his constitution was not equal to the demands of physical heroism. Nature had given him genius, but had denied the muscle. One can readily imagine him, like Shelley at Eton, beaten by a smaller boy; and if he had been silly enough to shoulder arms now in defence of his country we may be certain that he would have suffered more than he would have achieved. Chopin on the battlefield seems as much of an incongruity as a sailor on horseback. The material was hardly in him for fighting the battle of life, let alone the battle of nations.

What was the state of his feelings under this new crisis can easily be gathered from his letters. Writing to Matuszynski he says:

I would not willingly be a burden to my father; were I not in fear of that, I should at once return to Warsaw. I often feel that I curse the moment in which I ever left my home. You will, I am sure, feel for me in my condition, and understand that since Titus [Woyciechowski] went away too much has suddenly fallen upon me. The numerous dinners, soirées, concerts and balls, which I am obliged to be present at, only weary me. I am very melancholy, and feel so lonely and deserted here. There is no soul in whom I can unreservedly confide, yet I have so many 'friends.'

To the same intimate he appeals: 'Shall I go to Paris? Shall I return home? Shall I stay here? Shall I kill myself?' He must even send to Warsaw for guidance, worrying his parents about a decision which he ought to have made for himself. 'I do not know,' he says, 'whether I ought to go soon to Italy or wait a little longer. Please, dearest father, let me know your and my good mother's wish in this matter.'

The events of the time decided for him in regard to Italy, for the political disturbances which had now broken out in that country put all notion of a journey thither out of the question. Meanwhile he stayed on in Vienna, dwelling for the time being in a sort of castle of indolence. The following letter affords us a glimpse of the pleasant kind of life he was leading:

The intolerably stupid servant [1] calls me early, and I rise, take my coffee, which is frequently quite cold, owing to my forgetting my breakfast for my music. My German teacher appears punctually at nine o'clock, after which I generally write. Hummel [2] comes to work at my portrait, and Nidecki to study my concerto. I remain in my comfortable dressing-gown until twelve o'clock, at which hour Dr. Liebenfrost, a lawyer, sometimes drops in to see me, weather permitting. I walk with him on the Glacis, then we dine at the Böhmische Köchin, which is the rendezvous of the academy students, and afterwards we go to one of the best coffee-houses. Then I make calls, get into my evening clothes, and perhaps go to some soirée. About eleven or twelve o'clock (never later) I come home, play or read, and then go to bed.

In another letter he tells of having made the acquaintance of Dr. Malfatti, the emperor's physician-in-ordinary, who had

---

[1] At the house of Baroness Lachmanowicz, where he lodged.
[2] Son of the composer.

SIGISMUND THALBERG
After a Caricature by Dantan

attended Beethoven on his death-bed four years before. 'Malfatti really loves me, and I am not a little proud of it,' he writes. The doctor seems to have taken both a fatherly and a professional interest in him. The state of his health at this date cannot be precisely determined. He writes, indeed, to his parents that he is 'very brisk and in good health,' but it was a point of honour with him to conceal his troubles as much as possible from the home circle. At any rate we have the suggestive statement that 'Malfatti's soups have strengthened me so much that I now feel better than ever I did.' It is not unlikely that Beethoven's old friend detected the first inroads of the disease that was to cut him off while yet in his prime.

Of course, amid all the social and other diversions in which Chopin was engaged, his art was not forgotten. There was plenty of music to be heard—opera at the Kärnthnerthor Theatre, recitals by famous pianists, and so on. Special mention is made of Thalberg, who, born two years later than Chopin, was already famous as a technician. Naturally enough, perhaps, Chopin did not think so highly of him as the general musical public thought. For one thing, he was a Jew, and he disliked Jews as much as Wagner did. 'Thalberg,' he wrote, 'plays famously, but he is not my man. . . . He plays *forte* and *piano* with the pedals, but not with the hand: takes tenths as easily as I do octaves, and wears studs with diamonds.' The latter is a fine touch. Chopin could wield the dangerous weapon of irony as well as he could handle the pencil of the caricaturist. Witness also his verdict on Aloys Schmitt, whom he heard at this time: 'He is already over forty years old and composes eighty-year-old music.' He met also Slawik, the violin virtuoso, and Merk, the cellist, with whom he formed a trio. He heard Wild and Clara Heinefetter sing [at the opera, chiefly in works by Rossini, who was still the rage in Vienna]. About all these he has generally something interesting to say in his letters, though he seldom succeeds in saying anything very acute.

But this hearing of other people's music was not putting money in his purse, and the anxious father at home kept urging him to bestir himself and give a concert in order to replenish his resources. Chopin's only reply was that he had been too much discouraged to arrange about a concert. He played, however at a concert given by Madame Garcia-Vestris in April, when he was described, parenthetically, in the programme as 'pianoforte player'; and in June he met his parents' wishes by making a public appearance on his own account. For reasons which are not very clear now, the concert was a deplorable failure. Perhaps the cholera scare had something to do with it; perhaps also the political situation: Chopin was a Pole, and some of the better families may have stayed away from a prudent desire not to compromise themselves. The attendance at any rate was small, and the receipts fell greatly short of the expenses. It was another and a cruel blow to the young artist.

Soon after this we hear for the first time of Chopin being concerned about ways and means. Probably, as has been suggested, this was due to the failure of his recital; but, whatever the reason, he had now to submit to the humiliation of writing to his father for money to enable him to leave Vienna. Clearly it was not done without some pricks of conscience. 'I live as economically as possible,' he tells his people, 'and take as much care of every kreuzer as of that ring[1] in Warsaw. You may sell it; I have already cost you so much.' There is a spice

[1] Presumably the ring given to him by the Emperor Alexander. But why was he not wearing it? (The answer, surely, is patriotism. —E. B.)

of bitterness about this, not unnatural perhaps in the circumstances. But fate was not altogether to blame. Chopin's
letters abundantly prove that now, as later, he did not take
the care of the kreuzers that he might have done. Besides, he
ought to have been 'up and doing' before the kreuzers were
spent.

By this time, however, he had made up his mind to proceed
to Paris, and on 20th July 1831 he started on the journey,
with his friend Kumelski for companion. The Russian
Ambassador gave him permission to go as far as Munich,
where his further progress was barred by the non-arrival of
supplies from home. He took advantage of the enforced
delay to give a concert, aided by several fellow-artists, at which
he played the E minor Concerto and a Fantasy on Polish
Airs. This, on 28th August, was his last public appearance
before a German-speaking audience, and, although he liked
Germans as little as he liked Jews, it doubtless afforded him
some satisfaction in the retrospect that the press spoke very
highly both of his playing and his compositions. The
Germans, like the Viennese, 'do everything too tamely, in
a mediocre fashion which kills me.' But, as Balzac says,
praise agrees with the artist from whatever quarter it comes.

Leaving the Bavarian capital, Chopin next proceeded to
Stuttgart, where he was thrown into a state of consternation
by learning of the capture of Warsaw by the Russians, 8th
September 1831. He deeply loved his country, and this final
shattering of the hopes of the Polish revolution 'left a scar
which lasted indelibly.' It 'caused me very great pain—who
could have foreseen it?' he wrote. Count Tarnowski, in his
recollections, quotes some extracts from a diary which he is
said to have kept at the time. If the extracts are genuine—
about which there is more than a doubt, for the melodramatic

style is opposed to Chopin's usual manner—he must have been terribly agitated.

My poor father! [he writes]. My dearest ones! Perhaps they hunger? Maybe he has not anything to buy bread for mother? Perhaps my sisters have fallen victims to the fury of the Muscovite soldiers? Oh, father, is this the consolation of your old age? Mother, poor suffering mother, is it for this you outlived your daughter? And I am here with empty hands! Sometimes I groan, suffer and despair at the piano! O God, move the earth that it may swallow the humanity of this century! May the most cruel fortune fall upon the French, that they did not come to our aid!

And then the beloved one—the 'ideal,' Konstancja. 'What happened to her? Where is she? Poverty-stricken perhaps in the hands of the Muscovites; a Muscovite strangles her, murders her. Ah, my life! Here am I, alone. Come to me. I will wipe away your tears: will heal your wounds of the present by recalling the past.'

If Chopin did write this, there is a pathetic irony about that invocation of evil on the French; for it was towards France that Chopin's steps were now bent.[1] Poland's downfall sent him farther from her. He 'told his piano' how he felt about her misfortunes in the magnificent Study in C minor (Op. 10, No. 12), which has been well described as 'one of the truest and saddest utterances of despairing patriotism.'[2] For the present he buried his grief and set out to complete a journey which, as it proved, irrevocably fixed his fate. In the early days of October he arrived in Paris.

[1] His passport, however, was marked 'through Paris to London.' —E. B.

[2] It is not known whether this story is authentic.—E. B.

Disaster in Poland

So, practically, ends the first of the two chapters of Chopin's life. Warsaw, free, peaceful and happy: that is the first chapter; Paris, stormy, unconventional, charged with illness, charged with sorrow, closing with death: that is the second chapter. In the first Chopin is a boy, 'studying with his masters, secure under the protection of his home, and looking with expectant eyes upon a world of which he hardly knows the outskirts.' In the second he is the man, 'holding his fate in his own hands, living in a foreign city, surrounded with new hopes, new occupations and new friendships.' Poland is no more. She exists only in the chambers of memory and in the music, most of it as yet unwritten, of her famous son.

CHAPTER V

PARIS

LET us glance for a moment at this Paris of 1831 into which Chopin, the young man of twenty-one, was thus plunged. To Chopin it was, as he wrote, the place where one might have everything that he wanted—where 'you can amuse yourself, mope, laugh, weep, in short, do whatever you like. No one notices it, because thousands do the same.' So much might be said of the Paris of to-day, of any large city. But the Paris of 1831 was something more than a place where one might do whatever he pleased. It was still the scene of political ferment. Louis Philippe had been more than a year on the throne, and every section of the populace was divided into parties. As Chopin suggestively said, 'shabby individuals with wild physiognomies' were to be seen everywhere. The Polish insurrection had aroused general sympathy: dramas dealing with it were staged at several of the theatres, and shouts of *Vivent les Polonais* were being heard in the streets. Chopin probably paid but little heed to these things, for, as already remarked, he detested politics and was always impatient when the subject was discussed in his presence.

But Paris was notable for other reasons than for its political agitation. 'There is a host of interesting people here, belonging to the various professions,' said the young musician. That was putting it mildly. Think of the great names who were then associated with literature and art in the capital. This very year, as Niecks points out, had seen the publication of

Victor Hugo's *Notre-Dame de Paris,* of Dumas's *Charles VII,*
of Balzac's *La Peau de chagrin,* of George Sand's first novel,
Rose et Blanche. Only a year before Alfred de Musset,
'spoiled child of a world which he spoiled,' *l'enfant perdu* of
love, wine and song, and Théophile Gautier, the 'wild man'
of the romantic movement, had made their literary débuts.
Chateaubriand, Nodier, Béranger, Baudelaire, Mérimée,
Scribe, Sainte-Beuve, Vigny, Cousin, Michelet, Thiers,
Guizot—these and many others were busy with their pens
when Chopin arrived on the banks of the Seine. Heine,
too, was there—that strange enigmatic genius who 'dipped
his pen in honey and gall and sneered and wept in the same
couplet'—the Heine who wanted to ask Chopin if his muse
'still continued to drape her silvery veil around the flowing
locks of her green hair with a coquetry so enticing — if the
trees at moonlight always sang so harmoniously' as Chopin
sang on the ivory keys. Among the painters, again, there were
many celebrities. There was Eugène Delacroix, the Hugo of
the easel, who described Chopin as 'a man of rare distinction,
the truest artist I have met'; Ary Scheffer, who, from
genre pictures, was just about to turn to religious subjects;
Horace Vernet, whose battle pieces were 'delightful incense'
to that mean shadow of a real patriotism, French chauvinism;
Paul Delaroche, who so successfully united the picturesqueness
of the romantic with the dignity of the classic school, and
many more besides.

Most important of all to Chopin, there were the musicians.
Berlioz, as yet, was known practically only as a daring student,
having gone to Italy in 1830 as the winner of the Prix de
Rome. Cherubini, the grand old man of the profession—
'always speaking of cholera and the revolution,' said Chopin
—enforced his pedantic rules of harmony and counterpoint as

head of the Conservatoire. At that institution Lesueur was still teaching. Reicha, too, who, when he gave a lesson, 'looked at the clock all the time.' Hérold had just scored his greatest success with *Zampa*; Boieldieu and Paer were hoping to win fresh laurels; Auber, Rossini and Meyerbeer were the operatic gods of the time. Liszt was only beginning to compose, but already his astounding feats of technique and his dazzling personality had conquered the public and the fashionable world of Paris. Among the other players were Baillot, the violinist; Franchomme, the cellist, with whom Chopin was to form a close friendship; and Kalkbrenner, the pianist and professor, of whom more will be said presently. At the Italian opera might be heard such a galaxy of stars as Malibran-Garcia, Pasta, Rubini, Lablache, Tamburini and Schroeder-Devrient. [The Opéra had such great French artists as Mme Cinti-Damoreau, Mlle Dorus, Cornélie Falcon, Nourrit and Levasseur.] 'It is only here that one can learn what singing is,' wrote Chopin in the first days of his enthusiasm.

This was the Paris of 1831—the quintessence of art and literature, the home of fantasy and passion. Freedom was among the watchwords of the time, and the cry was: 'Away with the greybeards!' The triumph of romanticism, towards which a band of ardent and distinguished spirits had been striving for years, had recently been announced by the performance of Victor Hugo's *Hernani,* in which every tradition of the classical drama was violated with perhaps more audacity than real success. Henceforth the drama, poetry and literature in general were to be freed from the shackles imposed by the great writers of Racine's age, and the same forces which had wrought a revolution in politics and literature were beginning to find expression in music too.

Notwithstanding that he had passed the bar of criticism in Vienna and Berlin, to say nothing of Warsaw and the smaller towns where he had appeared, Chopin was still diffident about his attainments as a pianist. In fact he considered himself self-taught. 'I cannot create a new school, because I do not even know the old,' he said. Now that he had reached, as it were, the centre of musical civilization, among the first thoughts that occurred to him was that of perfecting his technique. Kalkbrenner was then the leading teacher of the piano in Paris. His 'enchanting touch' and the smoothness of his playing had commended him to the young Pole, and, having a letter of introduction in his pocket, he went to consult him about lessons. The 'gouty old gentleman' whom Heine, quoting Koreff, described as looking like a bonbon that had been in the mud, received him as kindly as his pompous manner would permit, heard him play, was rather taken aback by his 'unconstitutional effects,' and finally recommended a course of three years' study. The best account of the interview is given by Chopin himself in a letter to Woyciechowski. After remarking that he had played the E minor Concerto to Kalkbrenner, who told him that he had the style of Cramer and the touch of Field, Chopin continues:

He proposed to teach me for three years, and to make a great artist of me, but I do not wish to be an imitation of him, and three years is too long a time for me. . . . After having watched me attentively, he came to the conclusion that I had no method; that although I was at present in a very fair way, I might easily go astray, and that when *he* ceased to play, there would no longer be a representative of the grand old pianoforte school left.

Kalkbrenner was vastly conceited.

Chopin could hardly have given up three years to study with him, for he had his living to earn, and three years, as he

says, was too long a time. But here again his native indeter-
mination came into play: he was unable to decide for himself
what to do. In his perplexity he wrote to Elsner, his old
Warsaw master and friend. Elsner did not hesitate a moment.
Kalkbrenner, he replied in effect, would only destroy Chopin's
originality, even if he could really teach him anything on the
technical side. Moreover, he continued, piano playing was,
after all, but a minor branch of the art. Mozart and Beethoven
were pianists, but their greater accomplishments as composers
had quite overshadowed their achievements as masters of the
keyboard. 'In a word,' said Elsner, 'that quality in an artist
(who continually learns from what is around him) which
excites the wonder of his contemporaries can only arrive at
perfection by and through himself. The cause of his fame,
whether in the present or the future, is none other than his
own gifted individuality manifested in his works.' A genius
'should be allowed to follow his own path and make his own
discoveries.' Elsner had immense confidence in his pupil.
Not long after this he prompted him to try his hand at an opera.

Looking now at the respective positions of Chopin and
Kalkbrenner, one is disposed to regard his advice as eminently
sensible. The suggestion has been ventured that Kalkbrenner's policy was to keep Chopin in the background, and
that from motives of jealousy. But this need not be taken
seriously. It is only mediocrity that is jealous, and Kalkbrenner was no mediocrity. His proposal for a three years'
course of study was clearly made in good faith; and when
all is said and done there can be no question that Chopin,
genius as he was, would have learned not a little of the
technique of the keyboard from the elder master. Chopin's
friends asserted that his playing was better than Kalkbrenner's.
No doubt it was, though Chopin himself did not think so.

He declared that he could play as well as Herz, but Kalk-brenner 'is perfection in quite another style than Paganini's.' Some good authorities did not, indeed, think so highly of Kalkbrenner. Charles Hallé, for example, tells in his re-miniscences how he had gone to Kalkbrenner for lessons about five years later than this. At their first and, as it would appear, only interview Kalkbrenner played a composition of his own, 'one of the dullest pieces ever perpetrated. I admired the elegance and neatness of his scales and *legato* playing,' writes Hallé, 'but was not otherwise struck by his performance, having expected more, and wondering at some wrong notes which I had detected.' Two or three days later Hallé heard Chopin for the first time and was fascinated beyond expression.

It seemed to me [he says] as if I had got into another world, and all thought of Kalkbrenner was driven out of my mind. I sat entranced, filled with wonderment; and if the room had suddenly been peopled with fairies I should not have been astonished. The marvellous charm, the poetry and originality, the perfect freedom and absolute lucidity of Chopin's playing at that time cannot be described. It was perfection in every sense.

This is sufficiently corroborative of the contention of Chopin's friends that, as regards the effect produced on listeners, Chopin was infinitely the superior of Kalkbrenner. That much we should have assumed in any case. Nevertheless, there is abundant reason for believing that Chopin's system of fingering, to notice only one point, was not such as Kalkbrenner could possibly have approved. Moreover, that distinguished pro-fessor had a rule never to take pupils for a shorter period than three years. On the whole, therefore, one is constrained to say that Elsner was more jealous of Kalkbrenner than Kalk-brenner was jealous of Chopin. There is a natural tendency in one music master to imagine that he has done for a pupil all that another, however eminent, can do. (The reader will remember Thackeray's amusing description of the rivalry between Sir George Thrum and Signor Baroski.) The Warsaw musician was probably not altogether innocent of this weakness. Chopin, however, decided to follow his advice. Replying to his letter, he wrote: 'Although, as Kalkbrenner himself has admitted, three years' study is far too much, I would willingly make up my mind to even that length of time were I sure that in the end I should attain my object. But one thing is quite clear to me, and that is, that I shall never be a mere replica of Kalkbrenner.' Yet he experiences a momentary hesitation. Mozart and Beethoven, no doubt, were known chiefly as composers. But Spohr and Ries were composers mainly by virtue of their virtuosity, and why not he, too? This is a point upon which, fortunately, it is not necessary to enlarge.

The explanation of the whole matter, of course, is that Kalkbrenner was a classic, Chopin a romantic, if we may adopt terms then on everybody's lips. Relations of master and pupil between the two could not have lasted for six months. Kalkbrenner would have said: 'You must not do this or that'; and to Chopin's question 'Why?' he would have replied: 'Because Bach and Mozart and Haydn did not do it.' 'But I wish to do it; is it bad, unpleasant, in itself?' says Chopin. And Kalkbrenner would have been at a loss for an answer. The only thing that seems worth noting further is that Chopin, after a few lessons which he found an excuse for not continuing, perfected his technique by himself, and that he and Kalkbrenner continued on the most friendly terms, as is evidenced by reciprocal dedications of their works.[1]

[1] Chopin's E minor Concerto is dedicated to Kalkbrenner, and the latter wrote Variations on a Mazurka by Chopin.

Indeed, Kalkbrenner was one of those who had arranged to play at the young artist's first concert, to be given in Paris on 6th December 1831. I say had arranged, for, as a matter of fact, the concert was not given until 26th February 1832. First, there was some difficulty about a vocalist, then Kalkbrenner was suddenly taken ill. When the concert finally came off it was a financial failure, the audience consisting mostly of Polish refugees. Karasowski says there was scarcely a French person present. But the artistic success was undoubted. The programme included the F minor Concerto and the Variations on *Là ci darem,* and there was an appalling work of Kalkbrenner's, a March and Polonaise for six pianos, with the composer, Chopin, Hiller, Osborne, Stamaty and Sowinski all taking part. Sir Henry Hadow conjectures that Liszt, who was certainly present, was one of the pianists, and expresses regret that we do not know who was considered worthy to complete the sextet. But the names just mentioned are given by Chopin himself in a letter of the previous December, in which he discusses the arrangements for the concert. Of course, some of the six may have dropped out in the interval. [Another artist who took part in the concert was the violinist Baillot.]

The criticisms seem to have been entirely favourable. Liszt speaks of 'the most enthusiastic applause, again and again renewed.' Mendelssohn, who was annoyed at what he called Kalkbrenner's arrogance in proposing the three years' course of study, 'applauded furiously.' Hiller declared that after this nothing more was heard of Chopin's lack of technique. Even Fétis, the musical historian—of whom, said Chopin, one could learn much—descended from the high horse and shouted huzzas with the rest. Chopin's music revealed to him 'an abundance of original ideas of a type to be found nowhere else,' the 'indication of a renewal of forms which may in time exercise no small influence over his special branch of the art'; Chopin's playing he characterized as 'elegant, easy and graceful, possessing great brilliance and neatness.' In a word, though the young artist made no money by this first recital in the French capital, he made what proved ultimately much more valuable to him—a reputation.

On 20th May 1832 he gave his second concert, a charity affair organized by Prince de la Moskowa. At this he scored another artistic triumph, though the *Revue Musicale* echoed once more the plaint about 'the small volume of tone which M. Chopin draws from the piano.' But Chopin was beginning to find that artistic triumphs were not enough. Fame was all very well, but, to transpose a well-known saying of Sterne's, he had to write (and play), not to be famous, but to be fed. He had so far added nothing to his scanty financial resources, and at twenty-two he could not be continually calling on his father to replenish his purse. He had come to Paris with high hopes; already he was descending to the depths of despondency.

As usual, he unburdened himself to Woyciechowski. 'My health,' he wrote, 'is very bad. I appear indeed merry, especially when I am among my fellow-countrymen; but inwardly something torments me—a gloomy presentiment, unrest, bad dreams, sleeplessness, yearning, indifference to everything, to the desire to live and the desire to die.' How he represented the situation to his parents we have, unluckily, no means of knowing. His letters home, like his first piano and his portrait by Ary Scheffer, were destroyed by Russian soldiers in Warsaw in 1863;[1] but it is suggestive that Kara-

[1] The Chopin belongings were piled up, with other material, in the courtyard of the Zamoyskis' palace. 'Several pianos of

sowski, who saw them, says they were tinged with melancholy. Chopin seldom vexed his own people with tales of his misfortunes, and we may be sure that if he wrote dark letters to them at this time his dejection was extreme.

There is more than a hint of his condition, at least on the financial side, in the statement that he began to entertain the mad project of emigrating to America. Imagine Chopin in the America of 1832! According to the usual story, Chopin was only prevented from going there by a chance meeting with Prince Radziwill. The prince, it is said, took him to a soirée at the house of his friends the Rothschilds, where he played with such effect as to secure the promise of several well-paying pupils on the spot. Niecks questions the credibility of this anecdote, mainly on the ground that Liszt, Hiller, Franchomme and Sowinski never heard of it. But I am disposed to agree with Charles Willeby in thinking that Chopin's pride, to say nothing of the characteristic reticence of the Pole, may have led him to refrain from mentioning the incident to his friends. It was just the sort of kindness that a man of Prince Radziwill's good-nature was likely to have done him; and if we accept the story as authentic it will serve to explain, better than anything else, why Chopin remained in Paris after being so dissatisfied with his prospects as seriously to meditate crossing the Atlantic.

[It can hardly have been an affair of the heart which made

inferior Viennese make were cast out and killed by the fall. Chopin's piano, however, died hard. "It fell," says my informant, "with a loud melodious sigh, and I could not help admiring the solidity of Erard's workmanship when I saw that only its legs were broken."'—Sutherland Edwards in *Private History of the Polish Insurrection.* But Chopin's first piano was not an Erard: it was a Buchholtz. See Niecks, i. 246.

Chopin think of leaving Paris.[1] As his letter to Titus
Woyciechowski of 12th December 1831 shows, he cannot
be said to have fallen in love with the pupil and adopted
daughter or ward of Pixis, Franzilla Göhringer, a girl of
fifteen. Pixis, it appears, who was forty-three, was anxious
to marry the girl, and when Chopin paid him a visit, and was
discovered by him alone with Franzilla, something in the nature
of a scene from *The Barber of Seville,* with Pixis as Dr. Bartolo,
threatened to develop.] 'What do you think of this?' writes
Chopin. 'I, a dangerous *séducteur*!' The idea evidently
pleased him in a sportive kind of way. As Stevenson says,
nearly every man likes to be thought 'a bit of a rogue with
the women.'

The idea of transporting himself across the Atlantic was
dismissed entirely from his mind. Alike in society and as
a teacher he came speedily to the front. Pupils flocked to
him, invitations from this grand house and the other poured
in, distinguished visitors called, concert managers outbid
each other for his services. Liszt was then the society musician
in Paris, and Chopin began to encroach on his vogue. 'All
the Frenchwomen dote upon him, and all the men are jealous
of him,' said Orlowski. 'In a word, he is the fashion, and
we shall no doubt shortly have gloves *à la Chopin.*' Not so
very long after this, Jan Matuzynski, the young Polish doctor
who had just come to Paris as a professor in the School of
Medicine, looked him up and wrote home to say that 'Chopin
is now the first of pianists in Paris; he gives a great many
lessons, at twenty francs each, and is altogether in much
request.' Chopin's own account of the position shows how
quickly the dark clouds had been dispelled by the sunshine

[1] As the author suggested in the original edition of this book.—
E. B.

of success. This is how he writes to Dziewanowski in January 1833:

> I move in the highest circles, and I don't know how I got there. But you are credited with more talent if you have been heard at a soirée of the English or Austrian Ambassador. . . . Among the Paris artists I enjoy general esteem and friendship; men of reputation dedicate their compositions to me even before I have paid them the same compliment. Pupils from the Conservatoire— even private pupils of Moscheles, Herz and Kalkbrenner—come to me to take lessons, and associate my name with that of Field. Really, if I were even more silly than I am, I might imagine myself a finished artist; but I feel daily how much I have still to learn. . . . Don't imagine that I am making a fortune: my carriage and my white gloves eat up most of the earnings. However, I am a revolutionary and don't care for money.

This, we can see, is a rather different Chopin from the man who only two years before was writing to Woyciechowski: 'If I fail in my profession and wake up some morning to find myself without anything to eat, you must get a clerkship for me at Poturza. I shall be quite as happy in a stable as I was in your castle last summer.'

That, of course, was only a pleasantry. Chopin would never have been happy in a stable. Dainty surroundings and the intoxicating delights of success were more in his way than poverty and poor fare. Already he had provided himself with luxurious rooms, which he adorned with costly carpets and curtains, Venetian mirrors, all kinds of artistic treasures. He was extremely hospitable, especially devoting himself to compatriots, to whom he did the honours of Paris. He spent his money royally, drove about in a cab, wore white gloves, and so on. Indeed, the five years from 1833 to 1838 were perhaps the happiest period of his brief career. Lionized in society and received by the musical public with acclamation whenever he appeared, he tasted all the sweets of the artistic life, with hardly a single drop of bitterness to taint the draught. No doubt a dissentient voice was heard here and there, as when John Field growled out that he had 'a sick-room talent'; and Rellstab, the critic of the Berlin *Iris,* wrote of one of the mazurkas that 'had M. Chopin shown this composition to a master, the latter would have torn it up and thrown it at his feet, which we hereby do symbolically for him.' But such instances of vitriolic ill-nature were rare.

During 1833–4 he played a good deal in public and was constantly being heard in private. In December 1832 he had assisted, with Liszt, at a concert given by 'the good Hiller,' and shortly afterwards, in April 1833, he again appeared with Liszt at a performance for the benefit of Harriet Smithson, the bankrupt Irish actress whose charms had so captivated the inflammable Berlioz. He also played at a concert given by the brothers Herz. There was much private playing with Liszt and Hiller, and in some friendly contests with these and other artists Chopin was usually awarded the palm when Polish music was in question. In his livelier moods he would often sit down at the instrument and imitate his colleagues. This trick, to which reference will be made again, he played more especially on Thalberg, who said little, but evidently thought much. There is a story of Thalberg's going home with Hiller after a Chopin recital and starting to shout stentoriously on the way. The astonished Hiller demanded to know the reason of this aberration, and was told that a *forte* was absolutely necessary after having listened a whole evening to *pianissimo.* How these virtuosi loved one another, to be sure!

In the spring of 1834 Chopin went with Hiller to Aachen, where they attended the Lower Rhenish Musical Festival, held at Whitsuntide. They met Mendelssohn—then engaged on his *St. Paul*—at the festival, and all three proceeded to Düsseldorf, where Mendelssohn was at the time musical director. A very pleasant evening was spent at the house of F. W. Schadow, the head of the Düsseldorf Academy of Art. Hiller's account of the proceedings is worth reading. He says:

> The conversation soon became lively, and all would have been well had not poor Chopin sat so silent and unnoticed. However, both Mendelssohn and I knew that he would have his revenge, and was secretly rejoicing thereat. At last the piano was opened. I began, Mendelssohn followed, and then Chopin was asked to play, rather doubtful looks being cast at him and us. But he had scarcely played a few bars when every one present, especially Schadow, assumed a very different attitude towards him. They had never heard anything like it, and all were in the greatest delight, begging for more and more. Count Almaviva had dropped his disguise and all were speechless.

Mendelssohn seems to have genuinely liked Chopin, to whom, by the way, he gave the significant pet name of Chopinetto. Talking of a certain Prelude, he once said: 'It is so perfectly beautiful that I could go on for ever playing it over and over, all the more because by no possibility could I have written it.'[1] Of the meeting to which reference has just been made he wrote: 'Chopin is now one of the very first pianoforte players: he produces as novel effects as Paganini does on the violin and performs wonders which one would never have imagined possible.' The sole hint at criticism is found in the statement that Chopin was 'a little infected by the Parisian mania for despondency and straining after emotional vehemence.' For 'art with poisonous honey stolen from France' Mendelssohn had no great liking; but this

[1] C. L. Graves, *Life and Letters of Sir George Grove,* p. 366.

remark about Chopin meant nothing more than that he looked at his craft from a somewhat different standpoint. That Mendelssohn, as has sometimes been represented, opposed a determined front to Chopin's genius is as untrue as it is absurd. He was simply out of sympathy with certain ways in which that genius manifested itself.

After a short visit to Coblenz, Chopin returned with Hiller to Paris and resumed his teaching. He played at several concerts during the winter, once for Berlioz at the Conservatoire on 7th December 1834, twice for Pleyel, and once, on 5th April 1835, on behalf of the Polish refugees in Paris. [On 26th April he appeared at a concert given for the benefit of Habeneck by the Société des Concerts du Conservatoire, at which Cornélie Falcon and Nourrit sang. Here he played for the first time in the new *Andante spianato and Polonaise* for piano and orchestra (Op. 22), which had a great success.]

By this time Chopin had begun to conceive a dislike for platform playing. In private he always created something like a sensation, but the delicacy of his tone and his general style were not so suitable for the concert room. Hints to this effect were often being whispered in his ear by too candid friends, and their force was strengthened by an occasional frigid reception on the part of the public. If he had not already realized his own incapacity for the part of public virtuoso the fact was undoubtedly impressed on him later on. 'I am not at all fit for giving concerts,' he said to Liszt; 'the crowd intimidates me; its breath suffocates me; I feel paralysed by its strange look, and the sea of unknown faces makes me dumb.' Niecks represents this distaste of Chopin for the crowd, or rather his preference for the drawing-room, as 'a malignant cancer' which 'cruelly tortured and slowly consumed his life.' But that, as Sir Henry Hadow says, is an excess of eloquence. There is nothing to show that Chopin was in any way embittered by his inability to do himself justice on the concert platform. He certainly complained of being driven to the platform by financial necessity, but that is a very different thing from being distressed at finding himself unsuited by temperament for leading the kind of life that Liszt and Moscheles and other wandering heroes of the keyboard were leading. The world lost nothing by Chopin's dislike of the concert platform, and Chopin himself lost only a little of the world's material rewards. If he had played more in public it might have served as an advertisement for his compositions, to speak profanely, but in that case he would almost certainly have written less.

If we except an unimportant concert which followed shortly after, it was nearly four years from the date of the 1835 concert before Chopin again consented to face the public *en masse*. In the meantime he was going on with his teaching and with composition; was deep, as usual, in social engagements; and was making a host of new friends, musical and otherwise. An intimacy which gave him much pleasure was that which he formed with Bellini, for whose luscious melodies, especially in *Norma* and *I Puritani,* he had a peculiar fancy.[1] He has been sneered at for the preference; but though Bellini has now fallen into the background there is not wanting a certain similarity between his elegiac, idyllic style and the music of Chopin; and, as Stendhal sagaciously observed long ago, every eulogy between confrère and confrère is a certificate of resemblance.

[1] It was said that, just before his death, Chopin had expressed a desire to be buried beside Bellini. This was explicitly denied by Gutmann. He was, in fact, buried near Bellini, but that master's remains were removed in 1876 to his birthplace in Sicily.

In the summer and autumn of 1835 Chopin treated himself to a long holiday. First, he went to Carlsbad, where he met his father, whom he had not seen for nearly five years, and who was taking the waters there. Then he proceeded to Dresden, where he renewed his friendship with his father's old pupils, the Wodzinskis, who were now on their way back to Poland, after having resided in Geneva since 1830. Niecks has a passing observation about Chopin feeling the 'want of one with whom to sigh.' Chopin was something of an adept in the supplying of such a want. Here at Dresden at any rate he found one with whom to sigh—another 'ideal,' in fact. Her name was Marja Wodzinska,[1] and she was more than five years his junior. The particulars of this attachment are easily stated, for they have been set down by Count Wodzinski in his *Les Trois Romans de Frédéric Chopin.* The lady is described as tall and graceful, with features of 'indefinite charm.' 'Her magnificent hair,' we read, was silky and black as ebony; her nose 'somewhat pronounced'; and her face 'highly intelligent.' The precise heart relation-ships of the pair can, however, only be guessed. They met constantly for a month, and had much 'discoursing' of music together, and Chopin managed to get out of the transport a Waltz (A flat major, Op. 69, No. 1), which he afterwards sent from Paris, inscribed 'pour Mlle Marie.'

It is assumed that he made no positive avowal of his passion at this time, but waited until he met Marja at Marienbad the following summer. Karasowski says he 'soon discovered that Marja reciprocated his affection,' and that they were formally engaged, with the approval and consent of their relatives. Count Wodzinski, on the other hand, asserts that

[1] In Polish family names ending with 'i' the termination becomes 'a' when the name is applied to women.

the lady replied to the effect that, while her mother favoured the proposed union, her father objected on the score of Chopin's means and social position. The Wodzinskis, be it observed, were noble and wealthy, and pianists in those days did not make fortunes like those of more modern times. Karasowski hints at Chopin's desire to marry Marja and settle down to a quiet life in Warsaw. But this could have been rendered possible only by Marja's bringing her husband a fortune, and Marja, it is expressly stated, was not to become possessed of her estate until after the death of her parents. 'In love there are only beginnings,' said Madame de Staël. That was very likely the case with Chopin and Marja Wodzinska, [but there is little doubt that she actually engaged herself to him, pledging him to secrecy until her father's consent could be obtained. Whether this was refused or not, it is clear that she did not love him deeply, for in 1837 she wrote with such frigid politeness to Chopin that he had no choice but to regard the engagement, if indeed it had ever been made, as broken.] In 1841 she married Count Joseph Skarbek, the son of Chopin's godfather. Her marriage turned out so unhappily that it had ultimately to be dissolved. Some years later she consoled herself with a second husband—a Pole named Orpiszewski—and disappeared with him into obscurity. So ended another of the 'romances' of Frederic Chopin.

But to return. From Dresden, in the autumn of 1835, Chopin went on to Leipzig, where he made the acquaintance of Schumann and his future wife, Clara Wieck, Wenzel and others. Clara Wieck was then a girl of only sixteen, but her father had trained her so well that Chopin found in her at least 'one lady in Germany who could play his compositions.' He encountered Mendelssohn again, who proved, as he always did, 'the most genial of companions,' and protested himself 'enchanted anew' by Chopin's playing. Composers so seldom speak well of each other that it is interesting to note Schumann's comment on this visit. Writing to Heinrich Dorn, he says:

The day before yesterday, just after I had received your letter and was about to answer it, who should enter but Chopin? This was to me a great delight. We passed a very happy day together, in honour of which I made yesterday a holiday. . . . He played, in addition to a number of studies, several nocturnes and mazurkas —everything incomparable. You would like him immensely.

Chopin, unfortunately, did not reciprocate this cordiality, a cordiality reinforced by the practical efforts which Schumann made to popularize Chopin's compositions in Germany. Long before the general musical public awoke, Schumann had discovered and lauded Chopin. The 'Hats off, gentle-men: a genius!' with which Schumann greeted Chopin's Op. 2 is historical. But there was no enthusiasm, no appre-ciation on the other side. Chopin could praise Bellini; of Schumann's *Carnaval* he declared that it was really not music at all—surely one of the greatest of the many curiosities of musical criticism indulged in by composers. His pupil, Georges Mathias, told a good story in this connection. Schumann had sent to Heller a copy of the *Carnaval* for presentation to Chopin. It was luxuriously bound, with the title-page printed in colours. Heller handed it over to Chopin, who examined it and then remarked: 'How beautifully they get up these things in Germany!' Such a sally might have been expected from Rossini or Hans von Bülow; hardly from Chopin. The only satisfaction one's baser nature gets out of the matter is that Schumann wrote of the Chopin *Tarantella* (Op. 43): 'Nobody can call that music.'

Meeting with Schumann—Visit to London

Chopin continued his homeward journey via Heidelberg, reaching Paris in October 1835. The chief event of the following year was the visit to Marienbad already referred to, and in 1837, after the rupture with Marja Wodzinska, he paid a visit to London, in July. The latter was undertaken incognito, for what reason it is impossible to say. Accompanied by his friends Camille Pleyel and Stanislas Kozmian, Chopin passed under the name of 'M. Fritz.' He was introduced to James Broadwood, the famous pianoforte maker, as 'M. Fritz,' but his identity was betrayed as soon as he touched the keyboard. J. W. Davison, then editor of the *Musical World,* had the good fortune to hear him during this visit, and, contrary to expectation—for Davison was notoriously conservative and impatient of novelties—wrote a very eulogistic account of his performances. No record of Chopin's lodgings on the occasion seems to remain. It was a mysterious sort of visit altogether. Moscheles, writing of it in his diary, says that Chopin was 'the only one of the foreign artists who visited nobody and also did not wish to be visited, as every conversation aggravates his chest complaint. He went to some concerts and disappeared.' Mendelssohn, who was in London in August, also records that Chopin 'visited nobody and made no acquaintances.' Evidently he was really ill, and there may be something in Francis Hueffer's suggestion that he came to London to seek medical advice. He returned, after a short stay, to Paris, and next year he met the woman who more than any other influenced his life.

CHAPTER VI

No incident in the career of Chopin has occasioned more controversy, more miscellaneous writing, than his connection with George Sand. It has been discussed at portentous length by certain of his biographers; it has formed the subject-matter of a large number of essays, and a search through the back volumes of the leading magazines would probably bring to light a dozen or more articles all dealing with the debatable theme. It is a theme beset with difficulties of a peculiar kind, and one's first impulse is to shirk an examination of its details under the plea that an examination has been undertaken so many times already. But the biographer's duty seems plain. There is always a point of view. Estimates of the character of George Sand differ, and just as they differ, so do the constructions put upon her relations with Chopin. In a matter of this kind the individual reader must exercise his own judgment; and in order that he may exercise his judgment the necessary material must be presented.

'I have made the acquaintance of an important celebrity—Madame Dudevant, well known as George Sand, but I do not like her face; there is something in it that repels me.' Thus wrote Chopin to his parents immediately after the introduction. The composer's biographers are strangely at variance with each other as to the precise date and occasion of this introduction. Liszt, who was the friend of both

Chopin and George Sand, is positive in his statement that the meeting took place in Chopin's own apartments. More-over, he claims for himself the distinction of having arranged it at the express desire of the lady, whose curiosity had been aroused, not only by Chopin's compositions, but by the romantic stories she had heard of him. According to Liszt's version of the affair, Chopin declined to entertain the idea of an introduction, excusing himself on the ground of his aversion to literary women and his personal unfitness for their society. One morning, however, at the beginning of 1837, Liszt, finding Chopin in specially good spirits over some compositions he had just finished, persuaded him to have a little party in the evening. When the evening came, Liszt, without previous warning to Chopin, brought George Sand with him, and thus the introduction took place. Such is Liszt's story. George Sand agrees with it in the main, the only difference, indeed, being that she gives the credit of the introduction to the Countess d'Agoult,[1] who also accompanied Liszt on the occasion. There are other accounts of the introduction. Louis Énault says that it took place at the house of the Marquis de Custine, where most of the aristocracy of Europe assembled from time to time. His statement takes this picturesque form:

The last knots of the *chaîne anglaise* had already been united, the brilliant crowd had left the ballroom, the murmur of discreet conversation was heard in the boudoirs, and the fêtes of the intimate friends began. Chopin seated himself at the piano. He played one of those ballads whose words are written by no poet, but whose subjects, floating on the dreamy souls of nations, belong to the

---

[1] Subsequently known in literature as Daniel Stern. Chopin dedicated his twelve Studies (Op. 25) to her.

artist who likes to take them. Suddenly, in the middle of the ballad, he perceived, close to the door, immovable and pale, the beautiful face of Lélia. She fixed her passionate and sombre eyes upon him. The impressionable artist felt at the same time pain and pleasure. Others might listen to him. He played only for her. They met again. From this moment fears vanished, and these two noble souls understood each other—or believed that they understood each other.

Karasowski is rather more circumstantial. He says that the weather had affected Chopin's spirits, and that, thinking of something to dispel the depression, he set out for the house of the marquis at ten o'clock at night, on the *jour fixe* which always brought together an 'intellectual and agreeable company.' As he passed up the stairs he 'imagined himself followed by a shadow, exhaling an odour of violets,' and a presentiment as if something strange and wonderful were going to happen to him flashed through his mind. He was on the point of turning back when, 'laughing at his own supersitions, he sprang lightly up the remaining steps and entered the room.' Nothing remarkable occurred until most of the guests had left. Then Chopin seated himself at the piano and began to improvise. When he had finished he 'looked up and saw a simply-dressed lady leaning on the instrument and looking at him with her dark passionate eyes as if she would read his soul.' Chopin felt himself blushing under her fascinating gaze. She smiled slightly; and when he retired behind a group of camellias he 'heard the rustling of a silk dress and perceived the odour of violets.' In a 'deep, musical voice' the lady said a few words about his playing, remarking especially on his improvisation. Chopin was 'moved and flattered'—felt, in fact, that he was 'appreciated as he had never been before.' Thus Karasowski.

Adolf Gutmann, Chopin's favourite pupil, corroborates the essential facts of his statement, with the trifling variation that the marquis's company was not a chance assemblage but a musical *matinée*. Chopin, according to Gutmann, played a great deal during the evening, George Sand meanwhile devouring him with her eyes. He adds that the pair walked together a long time in the garden. There seems, on the whole, to be no reason for doubting that the two celebrities met at the Marquis de Custine's, but that they had their first meeting there is, in view of Liszt's declaration and George Sand's own statement, somewhat improbable. The point, fortunately, is not of capital importance.

Before going further it will help to a better understanding of the situation if we recall certain events in the previous career of George Sand. She had now been living for some years the life of a literary woman in Paris. Her marriage with Casimir Dudevant had turned out a failure, and the quiet monotony of the family residence at Nohant had become irksome to her. From the first husband and wife had been absolutely dependent on each other's society, and, being an ill-assorted pair, this solitude *à deux* became the reverse of advantageous. The only real link between them was their children, of whom, especially of her son Maurice, the mother was passionately fond. But this was not enough to compensate for the many disagreements that crept into the family life, and the end of it all was that Madame Dudevant 'threw her cap over the windmills,' practically gave up her home at Nohant, and settled down to earn her living in the capital. At first there had been some worry about finances, but George Sand was no longer in trouble on that score. Indeed, when she met Chopin she was a free woman, with full command of her original family resources, the courts having granted her a separation in 1836. Three years before this she had suddenly become enamoured of Alfred de Musset. The enchantment in that case was certainly mutual. She writes of herself as being lifted out of her previous depression and gloom by 'a happiness beyond any that she imagined, restoring youth to her heart.' But she was easily deceived. At this time Musset would, no doubt, have given all that he possessed to be able to make her his wife; but the infatuation was short-lived, the disillusion on both sides swift and complete. It was but a premonition of what was to happen in the case with which we are more immediately concerned. As one of her biographers has said, the man who won the heart of George Sand was not to be envied. She saw people often, as she confessed herself, through a 'prism of enthusiasm,' and afterwards recovered her lucidity of judgment, only to find that her self-delusion had led her into grave errors, upon which the world was likely to pass unsparing judgment.

Probably no two such opposites were ever drawn to each other as Chopin and George Sand. Not only in character but in physical constitution they were as dissimilar as could well be imagined. We have already gathered some notion of what Chopin was—neurotic, tender as a woman, dreamy, slim of frame, fragile. Contrast this with George Sand. Liszt speaks of her as an Amazon, a *femme héros,* who was not afraid to expose her masculine countenance to all suns and winds. Musset represents her as 'dark, pale, dull-complexioned, with glints as of bronze and strikingly large-eyed, like an Indian.' Heine, who must have been under her spell, said her face was beautiful rather than interesting, with features almost Grecian in their regularity. Others describe her as short and stout, dark and swarthy, with a thick and unshapely nose of the Hebraic cast, a coarse mouth,

GEORGE SAND

Engraving by H. Robinson after a Portrait by A. Charpentier

and a small chin. Clearly, on the physical side, not, we should have said, a woman to attract Chopin. What was on the other side? Brusque in her movements and 'natural' in her manners, George Sand had a horror of gloves and 'profound bows.' Social as well as ethical conventions she absolutely scorned. There is a well-known anecdote which pictures her pulling away at a cigar in the drawing-room of one of her friends. Seated beside a Russian gentleman whom she disliked, she was declaiming against the tyranny of his country, adding that in St. Petersburg she could not even smoke in a drawing-room. 'Madame, in *no* drawing-room have I ever seen any one smoke,' was the cutting reply. What the sensitive Chopin may have thought of these habits imagination could not easily exaggerate. His dislike of tobacco has already been noted in connection with his return journey from Berlin in 1828. James Huneker, commenting on the point, reminds us that one of the anecdotes related by Lenz accuses George Sand of calling for a match to light her cigar. 'Frédéric, un fidibus,'[1] she commanded, and Frederic obeyed. But there is a letter from Balzac to the Countess Hanska, dated 15th March 1841, which concludes: 'George Sand did not leave Paris last year. She lives at No. 16 Rue Pigalle. . . . Chopin is always there. *Elle ne fume que des cigarettes, et pas autre chose.*' The italics are in the letter. So much for Lenz and his *fidibus.*[2]

If we add to all this her eccentricities of dress, her taste for active amusements, her strong republican sympathies, her

---

[1] A spill.

[2] But there is also an earlier letter from Balzac, dated 2nd March 1838, in which he describes his finding her 'in her dressing-gown, smoking a cigar after dinner.' It looks as though Balzac implied in his later letter that she had given up cigars for Chopin's sake.—E.B.

emphatic disdain for rank and wealth, her lack of reticence, her impatience of moral restraints, her daring of so many things that others of her sex neither knew nor dared, we have surely a character so diametrically opposed to the character of Chopin that we may well wonder at the two names being associated in one of the most mysterious affairs of the heart to which nineteenth-century romance gave birth.

We have seen that Chopin disliked 'the woman with the sombre eye' (as Musset called her) when he first met her. Liszt speaks simply of his 'reserve'; but the feeling was much stronger than reserve. 'Yesterday I met George Sand,' says Chopin himself. 'She made a very disagreeable impression upon me.' Again, Ferdinand Hiller, in his *Open Letter to Franz Liszt,* writes: 'One evening you had assembled in your apartments the aristocracy of the French literary world. George Sand was, of course, one of the company. On the way home Chopin said to me: "What a repellent woman that Sand is! But is she really a woman? I am inclined to doubt it." ' Here, obviously, was sufficient antipathy to begin with. But a weak nature like Chopin's could not stand out against the virile charms of a George Sand. She had a splendid technique for overcoming masculine coyness; and the pair were soon seen together everywhere. Chopin had just been the hero of an unsuccessful wooing, and his heart being left, as we may suppose, bruised and empty, was no doubt, as it were, 'sensitized for the reception of a new impression by the action of love.' There is very little written evidence of the gradual growth of the passion between the two celebrities, but by the time it had reached its climax—that is, about the winter of 1838—we are able to follow it pretty clearly on the terra firma of documents. These documents are mainly from the pen of George Sand. Chopin never said much in writing about his private affairs. Moreover, his regular letters were nearly all addressed to his own family, and there were sufficient reasons for his keeping his illicit connection from their knowledge. How much or how little he told his people cannot now be said owing to the unfortunate destruction of his letters already mentioned. We can only accept the statement of Karasowski, who saw them, that the letters threw almost no light on the episode we are now considering.

After the victory in the French courts George Sand had resumed possession of Nohant, Dudevant having found another residence for himself. Chopin had meanwhile been ailing, and George Sand invited him to come and recuperate at Nohant. In 1837 we find her writing to Liszt: 'Tell Chopin that I beg of him to accompany you; that Marie [the Countess d'Agoult] cannot live without him, and that I adore him.' And again to the countess herself: 'Tell Chopin, whom I idolize, and all those whom you love, that I love them, and that brought by you they will be welcome.' These hearty invitations do not appear to have been immediately accepted by Chopin. Although there is no reliable information on the point, we may safely assume that he did not go to Nohant in 1837, but was there during the summer of 1838. His health was then becoming more precarious, and it was suggested by the doctors that he should spend the winter of 1838–9 in the south. This led to his going to the island of Majorca, with George Sand for companion.

Mystery again pursues us in regard to the arrangement of this visit. Liszt says that the intention was first formed by Chopin, and that Madame Sand, fearing to let him go alone, resolved to accompany him, avowedly in the character of nurse. Karasowski asserts, on the other hand, that it was George Sand who had decided to go to Majorca, and that she pressed Chopin to join her. In the account given by George Sand herself she says that when, in 1838, she was legally entrusted with the care of her son Maurice, who had hitherto been in the custody of his father, she decided to take him to a warmer climate, as he had been suffering from rheumatism. She had also another reason in the desire to secure for herself a period of quiet and leisure in order to study history and teach the children French. She goes on to say:

As I was making my plans and preparations for departure, Chopin, whom I saw every day, and whose genius and character I tenderly loved, said to me that if he were in Maurice's place he would speedily recover. I believed it, and I was mistaken. His friends had for long urged him to go and spend some time in the south of Europe. People believed that he was consumptive. Gaubert examined him and declared that he was not. 'You will save him, in fact,' he said to me, 'if you give him air, exercise and rest.' Others, knowing well that Chopin would never make up his mind to leave the society of Paris without being carried off by a person whom he loved, and who was devoted to him, urged me strongly not to oppose the desire he showed so apropos, and in a quite unhoped-for way. As time showed, I was wrong in yielding to their hopes and my own solicitude. It was, indeed, enough to go abroad alone with two children—one already ill, the other full of exuberant health and spirits—without taking upon myself a terrible anxiety and a physician's responsibility. But Chopin was just then in a state of health that reassured everybody. We were all hopeful. Nevertheless, I begged Chopin to consider well his moral strength, because for several years he had never contemplated without dread the idea of leaving Paris, his physician, his acquaintances, his room even, and his piano. He was a slave to habit, and every change, however small it might be, was a terrible event in his life.

In default of another, we may as well accept this account

of the circumstances which led to the Majorca visit, [without passing in review all the high-minded sophistries with which George Sand justified to herself her determination to break with another lover, Mallefille.] Chopin himself appears to have had some hesitation about setting out with a lady for companion. Only one or two of his most intimate friends were told of the arrangement, and when he wrote from the island he espcially requested that he should not be made the subject of Parisian gossip. It is easy to understand his disquietude. Chopin was never vulgar in word or deed, and he knew perfectly well that the connection he had now formed would suggest the vulgar liaison to many of his intimates and acquaintances. It is true, as James Huneker points out, that Paris, especially artistic Paris, was full of such situations. Liszt 'protected' the Countess d'Agoult, who bore him children, Cosima von Bülow-Wagner among the rest. Balzac was apparently leading the life of a saint, but his most careful student, Vicomte de Lovenjoul, has pricked that bubble once for all. Even Gustave Flaubert, the ascetic giant of Rouen, had a 'romance' with Madame Louise Colet, a mediocre writer and imitator of George Sand. But all this did not help to allay the qualms of Chopin, who might fairly be called a moralist.

There is no need to dwell on the details of the journey to Majorca.[1] It is sufficient to say that Chopin joined George Sand at Perpignan, and that they embarked there for Barcelona, whence the voyage was safely accomplished in another boat. The party reached Palma, the capital, in magnificent November weather. They were enchanted with the scenery of the island.

[1] In connection with this visit to the Balearic Islands, it is of interest to read C. W. Wood's *Letters from Majorca* (London, 1888).

Everything, wrote George Sand, is picturesque, 'from the hut of the peasant, who in his most insignificant buildings has preserved the traditions of the Arabic style, to the infant clothed in rags and triumphant in his *malpropreté grandiose,* as Heine said of the market women of Verona.' The character of the landscape, she continues, 'richer than that of Africa in general, has quite as much breadth, calm and simplicity. It is green Switzerland under the sky of Calabria, with the solemnity and silence of the East. . . . The country, nature, trees, sky, sea and mountains surpass all my dreams; it is the promised land.'

But scenery cannot make up for the lack of the ordinary comforts of life, and the delight of the first days was but short-lived. The people, it was discovered, were thievish, ready to give an orange for nothing, but demanding a fabulous sum for a coat-button. Palma, according to George Sand, was without a single hotel, and, as there were no habitable apartments in the town, the party had to establish themselves in a villa in the neighbourhood. Even here the dainty, finical composer had to gaze on whitewashed walls and use furnishings of the most primitive kind. At first he seems to have taken it all in good humour—nay, to have even liked it. Writing to his friend Fontana, 19th November 1838, he says:

I am at Palma, among palms, cedars, cactuses, aloes and olive, orange, lemon, fig and pomegranate trees, etc. The sky is like a turquoise, the sea is like lapis lazuli, and the mountains are like emeralds. The air? The air is just as in heaven. During the day there is sunshine, and consequently it is warm. Everybody wears summer clothes. During the night guitars and songs are heard everywhere and at all hours. In one word, a charming life. I shall probably take up my quarters in a delightful monastery in one of the most beautiful sites in the world: sea, mountains, palm trees, cemetery, church of the Knights of the Cross, ruins of mosques, thousand-year-old olive trees! Ah! my dear friend, I am now enjoying life a little more; I am near what is most beautiful. I am a better man.

But the romantically impressionable Chopin was soon to see this paradise in a different light. That George Sand's manuscripts took a whole month to reach the office of the *Revue des Deux Mondes,* and that her companion's piano was two months on the journey from Paris, were the least of the visitors' troubles. A rainy season of exceptional severity set in, and the villa, being rather too well ventilated, was soon rendered unfit for occupation. The plaster swelled like a sponge, and there being no fire-place, the house became, as George Sand puts it, 'like a mantle of ice on our shoulders.' Chopin, delicate as he was, and subject to violent irritation of the larynx, immediately felt the effects of the damp, and began to ail and cough. The fumes of the braziers, with which they tried to keep the house tolerably warm, only aggravated his condition.

I have been as ill as a dog [he writes to Fontana on 3rd December], in spite of eighteen degrees [centigrade] of heat, and of roses and orange, palm and fig trees in blossom. I caught a severe cold. Three doctors, the most renowned in the island, were called in for consultation. One smelt what I spat, the second slapped me where I spat from, and the third sounded and listened when I spat. The first said that I would die, the second that I was dying, the third that I had died already; and in the meantime I live as I was living.

From this time the party became an object of dread to the population, the report having got abroad that Chopin was suffering from consumption, which the Majorcans believed to be highly infectious. In the end the proprietor of the villa gave his tenants notice to quit, on the ground that, having carried contagion into his house, they threatened prematurely the lives of his family. This summary warning caused no regret, for the occupants of the wretched villa were already running the risk of being drowned in their rooms; but to move the invalid was a serious matter, especially in the dreadful weather and by such primordial means of transport as were available. Ultimately another resting-place was found in the disused Carthusian monastery of Valdemosa hard by, and the outcasts bade farewell to their old quarters, not before they had been forced to pay for the replastering and white-washing of the house, which the landlord held to be a necessary disinfection.

At the new abode it was only a case of out of the frying-pan into the fire. Incredible difficulty was experienced in getting a stove, wood, linen and one knows not what else. It took two months to make a pair of tongs. Worst of all, George Sand had 'almost to cook.'

The domestic [she writes] is a brute; bigoted, lazy and gluttonous; a veritable son of a monk (I think all are that). Happily, the maid whom I have brought with me from Paris is very devoted, and resigns herself to do heavy work; but she is not strong and I have to help her. Besides, everything is dear, and proper nourishment is difficult to get when the stomach cannot stand either rancid oil or lard. I begin to get accustomed to it; but Chopin is ill every time we do not prepare his food ourselves. In short, our expedition here is, in many respects, a frightful fiasco!

With his feeling for details, and the want of what George Sand calls a 'refined well-being,' Chopin naturally took a dislike to Majorca after a few days' illness. And the trouble was that his health, instead of improving, became gradually worse. Bronchitis, from which he had already suffered, was now followed by what appeared to be laryngeal phthisis. The stupid physician suggested bleeding, but George Sand, with an instinctive feeling that this would be injurious, disregarded the advice and continued her nursing as before. Chopin's one desire was to get away from the island as soon as possible, but in the meantime he was far too weak to travel, and when his strength returned a little it was found that the steamer was prevented by contrary winds from leaving the port. The misery of the situation is vividly pictured by George Sand in her *Un Hiver à Majorque*.[1] There were days when even she lost all hope and courage. The gossip of the islanders depressed and annoyed her. 'This consumptive person,' said these barbarians, speaking of her invalid charge, 'is going to hell—first because he is consumptive, and second because he does not confess. If he is in this condition when he dies, we shall not bury him in consecrated ground; and as no one will be willing to give him a grave, his friends will have to manage matters as well as they can.' The Majorcans had noted with the gravest suspicion that Chopin failed to attend mass. Liszt assures us that so long as his sickness lasted George Sand never left the pillow of him who 'loved her even unto death with an attachment which, in losing all its joys, did not lose its intensity, which remained faithful to her even after all its memories had turned to pain.' This, it is to be feared, was one of Liszt's romantic exaggerations.

[1] Chopin's letters from Majorca are comparatively cheerful: he refers but casually to his ill-health and not without humour to the annoyance of not receiving the piano that had been sent from Paris and was delayed until 15th January. But the correspondence ceases after the beginning of 1839 and is resumed only from Marseilles in March.—E. B.

Chopin

George Sand was not nearly so devoted to Chopin's pillow as that! Here is an extract from her *Histoire de ma vie*:

The poor, great artist was a detestable patient. What I had feared, but unfortunately not enough, happened. He became completely demoralized. Bearing pain courageously enough, he could not overcome the disquietude of his imagination. The monastery was for him full of terrors and phantoms, even when he was well. He did not say so, and I had to guess it. On returning from my nocturnal explorations in the ruins with my children, I found him at ten o'clock at night before his piano, his face pale, his eyes wild, and his hair almost standing on end. It was some minutes before he could recognize us. He then made an attempt to laugh, and played to us sublime things that he had just composed; or, rather, to be more accurate, terrible and heart-rending ideas which had taken possession of him, as it were without his knowledge, in that hour of solitude, sadness and terror. It was then that he composed the most beautiful of those short pieces he modestly entitled *Préludes*. They are masterpieces. Several present to the mind visions of the dead and the sounds of the funeral chants which beset his imagination; others are melancholy and sweet. They occurred to him in the hours of sunshine and health, with the noise of the children's laughter under the window, the distant sound of guitars, the warbling of the birds among the humid foliage, and the sight of the pale little full-blown roses on the snow.

Chopin continued to grow worse; and, at last, towards the middle of February, the weather having improved, the party resolved to fly from Majorca at any risk. The lady, as already stated, had declared the sojourn to be 'a frightful fiasco'; and such it certainly was in the case of the invalid, who had arrived with a cough and now departed spitting blood. The passage from Palma to Barcelona was made under conditions which did not tend to improve matters. 'We were in company of a hundred pigs,' says George Sand, 'whose continual cries and foul smell left our patient no rest and no respirable air.' The haemorrhage continued all the way to Barcelona. There, happily, the misfortunes of the travellers were somewhat mitigated. A French ship's doctor was found who succeeded in stopping the bleeding from the lung within twenty-four hours. Chopin gradually got better, and, after resting for a week, the party set out for Marseilles, where they arrived at the end of February 1839. They saw Genoa for a few days—all that Chopin ever saw of the Italy which was at one time a passion with him, [and then settled down at the Hôtel de Beauvau in Marseilles until 22nd May. There Chopin's health gradually improved,] but at first he still required careful nursing, and it is evident that he was giving his companion some anxiety. Here is another extract from the *Histoire de ma vie* which will be read with interest for several reasons:

I asked myself if I ought to entertain the idea which Chopin had formed of taking up his abode near us. I should not have hesitated to say 'No' had I known then for how short a time the retired life and the solemnity of the country suited his moral and physical health. However, I entertained eventually the idea that Chopin might rest and regain his health by spending a few summers with us, his work necessarily calling him back to Paris in the winter. Nevertheless, the prospect of this kind of family union with a newly-made friend caused me to reflect. I felt alarmed at the task I was about to undertake, and which I had believed would be limited to the journey to Spain. A kind of terror seized me in presence of this new duty. I was not under the illusion of passion. I had for the artist a kind of maternal adoration, which was very warm, very real; but which could not for a moment contend with maternal love, the only chaste feeling which can be passionate. I was still young enough [George Sand was at this time thirty-five] to have perhaps to contend with love, with passion properly so called. The contingency of my age, of my situation and of the destiny of artistic women—especially when they have a horror of passing diversions—alarmed me much; and, resolved as I was never to submit to any influence which might divert me from my children, I saw a less but still possible danger in the tender friendship with which Chopin had inspired me. Well, after reflection, this danger disappeared, and even assumed an opposite character—that of a preservative against emotions which I no longer wished to know. One duty more in my life (already so full and so overburdened with work) appeared to me, one chance more to attain the austerity towards which I felt myself attracted with a kind of religious enthusiasm.

In later life George Sand thought that if at this period she had shut herself up alone at Nohant all the year round she would have saved Chopin from the danger which, unknown to her, threatened him—the danger, that is, of attaching himself too absolutely to her. She did not—so she declares—consider his affection exclusive, and her avowed belief was that it was not so great but that absence would have entirely cured him of the infatuation. If this was really her belief, it is a pity that she did not act on it.

Late in the autumn of 1839, after months spent at Nohant, Chopin did indeed go to Paris, but he did not go alone: George Sand went too. At first they lived apart, [she in the Rue Pigalle, he in the Rue Tronchet;] but the companion of the Majorcan visit tells us that Chopin's rooms were cold and damp, that he felt sorely the separation from her, and that she therefore agreed to their once more living together. Here is her own statement:

He again began to cough alarmingly, and I saw myself forced to give in my resignation as nurse, or to pass my life in impossible journeyings to and fro. Seeing how he took to heart his exclusion from our family life, I offered to let him one of the *pavillons*,[1] a part which I could give up to him. He joyfully accepted. He had there his room, received there his friends, and gave there his lessons, without incommoding me.

And so the years went on—Chopin regularly at Nohant during the summer for the next few years, [except in 1840, when he did not leave Paris.] George Sand asserted that he did not care for the monotony of country life, that he loved it only for a fortnight, after which he bore it simply out of regard for her. When his malady grew worse, she says his return to Nohant in the spring still filled him with ecstatic joy. But the joy was of short duration. As soon as he began to work, everything around him assumed a gloomy aspect. How much of this was due to the company, how much to an inherent dislike of the country, one cannot say. Liszt remarks that Chopin had often to put up with company which did not please him at all, as indeed may well be imagined. There is a very interesting letter written from Nohant by a Mlle de Rosières, a pupil of Chopin's. It runs thus:

Love is no longer here, at any rate on one side, but there is tenderness and devotion, mingled according to the day with regrets, gloom, ennui, affected by all sorts of causes, and especially by the clash of their dispositions, the divergence of their tastes, their opposed opinions. . . . She speaks to him sometimes too plainly, and that hurts him. On his side, he has his crazes, his vivacities, his antipathies, his exigencies, and he evidently has to give way, because she is what she is, and he hasn't the strength to fight. . . . In the evening her brother came to make a racket; and, heavens! what a racket! We all had our heads split with it. You'd fancy he was going to smash the billiard table: he throws the balls into the air, yells,

---

[1] One of the two little houses she had rented in the Rue Pigalle.

jumps about on his iron-tipped boots; and as Madame Sand says, he is tolerated because no one is bound to tolerate him. If one were, it would be a torture. He is by no means clean, and he is coarse in his talk. And he is nearly always drunk. It is said that the house was filled with people of that sort before Chopin's reign. . . . Chopin calls her his angel, but the angel has big wings that sometimes hurt you.

This letter serves the double purpose of showing the kind of thing that Chopin had to put up with at George Sand's Liberty Hall, and the fact that a certain coolness was already manifesting itself on the side of the 'angel.' But Chopin was a child of moods, and we must not make too much of the jarring notes at Nohant. In Paris he 'always wished for Nohant,' and when he got there he 'never could bear it.' That is simply the artistic temperament in combination with physical ill-being. A robust nature and a robust constitution would have enjoyed Nohant and its boisterous brusqueries.

We come now to what is really the most interesting part of this 'episode in the life of an artist.' Chopin's several biographers have done their best, but with small success, to unravel the mystery of his rupture with George Sand, an event which he himself regarded as one of the most momentous crises in his life. The published statements on the point are hopelessly contradictory. Some are untrustworthy on the face of them, and George Sand's own account must be regarded with some suspicion because of her self-interest. She gave a thoroughly misleading account of the Musset affair in *Elle et lui*; and, as Henry James has shown, she is never to be accepted without corroboration. Nevertheless, it is right that one of the leading characters in the little drama should be heard. Once more we draw from the *Histoire de ma vie*:

After the relapses of the invalid, his mind had become extremely gloomy, and Maurice,[1] who had hitherto tenderly loved him, was suddenly wounded by him in an unexpected manner about a trifling subject. They embraced each other the next moment, but the grain of sand had fallen into the tranquil lake, and little by little the pebbles fell there, one after another. All this was borne; but at last one day, Maurice, tired of the pin-pricks, spoke of giving up the game. That could not be, and should not be. Chopin would not stand my legitimate and necessary intervention. He bowed his head, and said that I no longer loved him. What blasphemy after these eight years of maternal devotion! But the poor bruised heart was not conscious of its delirium. I thought that some months passed at a distance and in silence would heal the wound, and make his friendship again calm, and his memory equitable. But the revolution of February came, and Paris became momentarily hateful to his mind, incapable of yielding to any commotion in the social form. . . . I saw him again for an instant in March 1848. I pressed his trembling and icy hand. I wished to speak to him; he slipped away. Now it was my turn to say that he no longer loved me. I spared him this infliction, and entrusted all to the hands of Providence and the future. I was not to see him again. There were bad hearts between us. There were good ones too, who were at a loss what to do. There were frivolous ones, who preferred not to meddle with such delicate matters. I have been told that he asked for me, regretted me, and loved me filially up to the very end. It was also thought fit to conceal from him that I was ready to hasten to him.

Thus George Sand. Liszt says that no one really knew what was the cause of the rupture. 'One saw only that, after a violent opposition to the marriage of the daughter of the house, Chopin precipitately left Nohant, never to return.' Karasowski, again, says that George Sand simply grew tired of her nursing and of the invalid's peevish complaints, and

---

[1] Maurice Dudevant, George Sand's son.

at last, when she found it impossible to effect a separation by cold looks and petty slights, she 'resorted to the heroic expedient' of caricaturing Chopin in a romance. Wodzinski also declares that the romance was the cause of the rupture—that the other alleged reasons were only a pretext.

And this brings us face to face with the vexed problem of whether *Lucrezia Floriani* was written, as Karasowski and others contend, with the express purpose of forcing a quarrel with the composer. Leaving aside the question of purpose in this instance, there can be no doubt that George Sand did make 'copy' out of her friends. The ethics of such a practice—a practice common enough with novelists—are difficult to define, and we need not stay to consider them. Heine once said that whenever a woman wrote a book she wrote with one eye on her manuscript and the other on a man. The question here is, did George Sand have her eye on Chopin when she drew the portrait of Prince Karol in *Lucrezia Floriani*? She gave a categorical denial to the charge of portraiture. But it is impossible to get over the fact that Chopin's friends all recognized the portrait. Nay, several of his biographers, Liszt among them, have tacitly admitted its authenticity by using a great part of the novelist's material in describing the real Chopin.

So much, I think, we are bound to allow. At the same time, it seems doubtful whether Chopin himself discovered his identity with Prince Karol. *Lucrezia Floriani,* as Sir Henry Hadow points out, was written during the winter of 1846, and was read by Chopin, chapter after chapter, as it proceeded. If, then, Chopin had taken offence at the book, the rupture would have occurred, as Karasowski positively asserts that it did, 'in the beginning of 1847.' This was certainly not the case. Chopin, who spent the spring in Paris, was in friendly correspondence with George Sand in May, and paid his usual visit to Nohant in the summer. We can hardly suppose that he would have offered himself as a guest to the woman whom he believed to have held him up to ridicule.

But the suggestion does not seem outrageous that Chopin may have read the book so listlessly as not to recognize himself in it. His literary perceptions were not very keen, and fiction, so far as I can make out, was not much to his taste. Wodzinski says that his eyes were opened by candid friends, who made it clear to him that his 'angel' had intentionally fooled him. The statement is probably a venture; but whether we accept it or not, it would be absurd to assert, as some writers have done, that Frederic Chopin and Prince Karol resembled each other only in 'a few superficial accidents' of portraiture. The resemblance is much closer than that.

Still, I am not entirely satisfied with the *Lucrezia Floriami* explanation of the quarrel. Sir Henry Hadow offers another, which seems to me to be the simplest and the most credible of the many conflicting versions of the story. According to this reading, the occasion of the estrangement was a quarrel with Maurice, the causes of which, though nowhere explicitly related, are not difficult to divine. George Sand had adopted a distant cousin called Augustine Brault, a quiet, colourless, inoffensive girl, whom she had rescued from the influences of a bad home. Maurice was fond of his cousin; Chopin disliked her, and rather unreasonably resented her appearance as an intrusion, thus making Maurice in turn regard him as an intruder. Again, in May 1847, occurred the marriage of Solange Dudevant with the sculptor Jean-Baptiste Clésinger, a marriage of which, at the time, Chopin alone disapproved. 'We can well imagine,' to quote Sir Henry Hadow, 'the words of pointed criticism and disdainful rejoinder, the interchange of sharp retorts, the gradual development of a contention which, as we know, culminated in Maurice's threat to leave his home. George Sand tried to make peace: Chopin, barely recovered from a new attack of illness, regarded her interference as an act of hostility; and after a few words of bitter reproach, "the first," she says, "which he ever offered me," he turned and left her in open anger.'

I have called this the simplest and most credible explanation of a perplexing affair. But, again, I am not prepared to say that other causes may not have contributed to the quarrel. The quarrel itself was inevitable—or at least if not a quarrel, a radical change in the relationships of the pair. In the first place, George Sand's coarse tastes must have clashed at every point with Chopin's. A man of his refined nature was bound to cut himself adrift from a woman of her character sooner or later. George Sand was a cormorant, quite unfit as a mate for a man like Chopin. The fire must have gone out eventually. In the second place, it was George Sand's way to close one 'romantic' valve abruptly while opening, or preparing to open, another. She cast her admirers aside, like a squeezed orange, when she had exhausted their emotional and psychological 'possibilities.' The Alfred de Musset affair has been mentioned. Musset had gone to Venice with George Sand. He fell ill, and his brother afterwards averred that his illness was aggravated by 'the unexpected vision of George Sand coquetting with the young medical man called in to prescribe for Alfred.' This is known as the Dr. Pagello incident. There were many such affairs.

[In the summer of 1847, after Chopin's return to Paris from Nohant, a terrible scene occurred there. Solange accused Augustine, who had in the meantime become engaged to Théodore Rousseau, of having been Maurice's mistress.

Quarrels and Separation

George Sand was furious with her daughter and there was a violent quarrel between Clésinger and Maurice, who took sides, the former with his wife, the latter with his mother. Solange then went to Paris and won Chopin over to her side, whereupon her mother broke with her lover in a letter which Delacroix, to whom Chopin showed it, admitted to be cruel. In August George Sand coldly inquired after Chopin's health through a friend, but professed to have no cause to regret the loss of his affection. He, on the other hand, was greatly hurt.] 'I would overlook all,' he wrote, 'if only she would allow me to stay with her at Nohant.' And again, in a letter to Gryzmala from London, dated 17th November 1848: 'I have never cursed any one, but now I am so weary of life that I am near cursing Lucrezia[1] [George Sand]. But she suffers too, and suffers more because she grows older in wickedness. What a pity about Sol![2] Alas! everything goes wrong in this world!'

Early in 1848 George Sand voluntarily sought a reconcilia-tion, but was repulsed. Only once, as she says herself, did she meet Chopin after the rupture, and he escaped without uttering a word. She called when he was dying, and was denied admission, though Chopin had told Franchomme two days before how 'she said to me that I would die in no arms but hers.' Perhaps she suffered unjustly, but one cannot help entertaining the suspicion that there was some real ground on Chopin's side for the persistent manner in which

[1] It looks very much as though Chopin, by this time at any rate, had been well enough aware of the significance of *Lucrezia Floriani* and his part of Prince Karol in it.—E. B.

[2] 'Sol' is Solange, who was forced to leave her husband because of ill-treatment. She was a clever woman, and wrote a book, *Masques et bouffons*. She died in 1899; Maurice in 1883.

he ignored her and kept her at a distance. It was she who said that he had no hatreds. Clearly, for her he had no forgiveness. The general opinion is that his end was hastened by the estrangement. 'As a wine too spirituous shatters the fragile vase, so George Sand shattered the frail and delicate Chopin.' That is how it is put by Liszt, who remarks further that the delicacy of Chopin's heart and constitution 'imposed upon him the woman's torture—that of enduring agonies never to be confessed; thus giving to his fate some of the darker hues of feminine destiny.' Lenz avers that Chopin really died of a broken heart. It is not necessary to go so far. Chopin's early death was in any case physically inevitable. At the most it can be said that the George Sand affair under-mined his feeble health.

CHAPTER VII

PARIS AGAIN

I HAVE thought it better to treat the George Sand episode by itself without mixing it up with the concurrent events of Chopin's career. It will now be necessary to return for a very brief narrative of his doings up to 1848, when he left Paris on his visit to England and Scotland. These last years of his life were singularly destitute of interesting incidents. The period is barren of details in all the biographies, even in the extensive work of Frederick Niecks.[1] As Jules Janin said, he 'lived ten miraculous years with a breath ready to fly away.' He became more inaccessible than ever, and, in consequence, has been described by some who knew him only then as snobbish and exclusive. But the state of his health explains everything—at least everything that is not otherwise accounted for by his retiring nature and his sensitive Slav temperament. It explains his comparatively few public appearances, and it explains his restriction in the matter of creative output. All through, his health was fluctuating—now better, now worse. And with this variation there was the inevitable change of mood. On his better days, to quote Sir Henry Hadow, he would be 'buoyant, gay, even extravagant, playing fantastic tricks at the pianoforte, or mimicking his rivals with inimitable skill and good-natured satire: on his worst he would appear peevish and fretful, not from ill-humour, but from sheer exaggeration of sensibility.' During

[1] The letters, too, are singularly devoid of interesting biographical facts.—E. B.

this period he had a serious quarrel with Liszt, which was never made up; and he 'broke into fierce anger at a stupid joke of Meyerbeer's which a moment's thought would have allowed him to disregard.' These things were mainly the outcome of his exaggerated sensibility acting through his enfeebled constitution. Unless we recognize this we shall do him a serious injustice. He was naturally of a genial, kindly temperament, but he would not have been the artist he was if he had not been keenly affected by the distressing physical condition in which he found himself.

In the winter of 1839 Chopin played at the court of Louis Philippe at Saint-Cloud, the leading work performed being Moscheles's Sonata in E flat major for four hands. Moscheles himself was the second player. The king presented Chopin —who was admired and petted like a favourite by the royal circle—with a gold cup and saucer in memory of the occasion, while Moscheles received a travelling case. 'The king gave him this,' remarked the malicious Chopin, 'to get rid of him the sooner.' Of course, the sally may have been uttered in a spirit of genuine amiability. But one is suspicious on the mere ground that Moscheles was a Jew. On Moscheles's side at any rate the relations of the two seem to have been as cordial as could reasonably be expected. Something of this was no doubt due to the fact that, by Moscheles's own testi-mony, Chopin declared that he 'loves my music very much, and at all events he knows it very well.' It was now that Moscheles, having heard Chopin play for the first time, came to understand his music, and could explain to himself the enthusiasm of the ladies. 'He is unique in the world of pianists,' was his verdict. Evidently he saw Chopin in one of his gayer moods, for he tells that he was 'exceedingly comical in his imitations of Pixis, Liszt and a hunchbacked

pianist.' These exhibitions appear to have been a feature of
his merry moments.

In 1840, as we have already seen, Chopin passed most of
his time in Paris. It is said that it was from motives of
economy that George Sand did not go to Nohant that summer.
On 26th April 1841 he gave a concert at Pleyel's rooms,
assisted by Madame Cinti-Damoreau, a distinguished operatic
artist, and Ernst, the violinist, who played his famous *Elégie*.
Liszt has an account of the function: 'Last Monday, at eight
o'clock in the evening,' he says, 'M. Pleyel's rooms were
brilliantly lit up; numerous carriages kept bringing to the foot
of the staircase, covered with carpet and perfumed with flowers,
the most elegant women, the most fashionable men, the most
celebrated artists, the wealthiest financiers—in fact, a whole
élite of society; a whole aristocracy of birth, fortune, talent and
beauty.' It does not seem to have been a public audience in
the ordinary sense, but rather a gathering of friends and
admirers who, as Chopin told Lenz, 'took the tickets in advance
and distributed them among themselves.' Chopin, at any
rate, was received with the utmost enthusiasm—'overwhelmed
with bravos,' says one of the papers. He was three times
encored and, according to Liszt, would have been asked to
repeat every item on the programme had it not been for his
evident weakness. The criticisms quoted by Niecks are all
interesting for one reason or another; the following from *La
France musicale* is specially so for its summing-up of Chopin's
essential qualities as a player and composer:

Chopin is a composer from conviction. He composes for himself, and what he composes he performs for himself. . . . Chopin
is the pianist of sentiment *par excellence*. One may say that Chopin
is the creator of a school of piano playing and of a school of composition. Indeed, nothing equals the lightness and sweetness with

which the artist preludes on the piano; nothing again can be placed by the side of his works, full of originality, distinction and grace. Chopin is an exceptional pianist who ought not to be, and cannot be, compared with any one.

Encouraged by the success of this concert, Chopin made another appearance in the same rooms on 21st February 1842, when Pauline Viardot-Garcia and the cellist Franchomme, a great personal friend of his, took part. There was again a brilliant audience. In this connection it is impossible to resist quoting the following from the report of the concert in *La France musicale*:

Chopin gave in Pleyel's hall a charming soirée, a fête peopled with adorable smiles, delicate and rosy faces, small and well-formed white hands; a splendid fête where simplicity was combined with grace and elegance, and where good taste served as a pedestal to wealth. Those ugly black hats which give to men the most unsightly appearance possible were very few in number. The gilded ribbons, the delicate blue gauze, the chaplets of trembling pearls, the freshest roses and mignonette, in short, a thousand medleys of the prettiest and gayest colours were assembled, and intersected each other in all sorts of ways on the perfumed heads and snowy shoulders of the most charming women for whom the princely *salons* contend.

George Sand was present at this concert, 'the observed of all observers.' For the rest, it is sufficient to note the aristocratic character of the audience and the preponderance of ladies—a feature of all Chopin recitals.

In 1844 Chopin was prostrated by the death of his father, who succumbed to chest and heart complaints. He lay very seriously ill for a fortnight, carefully tended—to her credit be it said—by George Sand, who wrote his letters to his mother and summoned one of his sisters from Warsaw. When he could be moved she carried him off to Nohant, where he soon made a temporary recovery. The years 1845 and 1846 passed almost without incident of any kind. In 1845 he published the *Berceuse* and the Sonata in B minor; in 1846 the *Barcarolle,* the *Polonaise-Fantaisie,* and a few mazurkas and nocturnes; but 'even in his art the record is meagre, and in his life it is almost non-existent. We have half a dozen unimportant letters, we have half a dozen lines of anecdote or conjecture, and the rest is silence.' In 1847 came, as we have seen, the rupture with George Sand, after which we march slowly and sadly to the end.

In 1848 Chopin, driven to that detested expedient by lack of means, gave what proved to be his last concert in Paris. It took place on 16th February. He had been obliged by sheer want of strength to curtail his teaching, often giving lessons to such pupils as he retained while lying on a couch, with a second piano at hand for illustration. It must have been a heavy trial for him to face the crowd in this enfeebled condition, and one thinks all the more of his heroism—it can be called nothing less—because he had at the time several manuscripts which, had he been less rigid in his self-criticism, might have been published in relief of his immediate needs. He has been mildly censured for the tradesman-like way in which he stuck out for his prices with the publishers. But this at least should be remembered to his credit, that he never asked the publishers to pay him for compositions which he deemed unworthy of his powers. His Sonata in G minor for cello and piano, published at this time, was the last work which he allowed to be given to the world.

Of the Paris concert there is no occasion to say much. In the programme were found the names of Alard, Franchomme, Mlle di Mondi and Roger; while the musical items included, beside the new cello Sonata, such of Chopin's works as the

Barcarolle and *Berceuse,* and several of the smaller pieces, nocturnes, preludes and studies. The scene was a repetition of those already described, the ladies being there again in 'colours gayer than the morning mist'; but the fact that this was Chopin's last appearance in a city with whose artistic life he had been so long associated justifies the following quotation from the *Gazette musicale*:

A concert by the Ariel of pianists is a thing too rare to be given, like other concerts, by opening both wings of the door to whosoever wishes to enter. For this one a list has been drawn up; every one inscribed thereon his name; but every one was not sure of obtaining the precious ticket. Patronage was required to be admitted into the holy of holies. . . . The outcome of all this, naturally, was that the fine flower of the aristocracy of the most distinguished women, the most elegant toilettes, filled Pleyel's rooms on Wednesday.

Doubt has been expressed by Niecks and others as to the selection of the audience here indicated. There seems to be no question about it. Otto Goldschmidt, the husband of Jenny Lind, was present at the concert, and at a meeting of the London Musical Association in April 1881 he said: 'It was extremely difficult to obtain admission, for Chopin, who has been truly described as a most sensitive man, not only had a list submitted to him of those who ought to be admitted, but he sifted that list and made a selection from the selected list.' Goldschmidt further remarked that while Chopin was evidently extremely weak, his playing, 'by reason of that remarkable quality which he possessed, of gradation in touch, betrayed none of the impress of weakness which some attribute to softness of touch.' Another who was present stated that Chopin, though looking pale, did not seem to be so ill as has been generally supposed. Probably he made a special effort to brace himself for the occasion. When it was all over he broke down completely and nearly fainted in the artists' room.

A week later—on 22nd February 1848—the Revolution broke out, and Chopin wisely deemed it expedient to leave Paris with as little delay as possible. Other reasons have been suggested for his departure, but while he, no doubt, availed himself of the political situation to carry out an old promise to revisit England, it would have been in any case only prudent to leave a city in which violence and mob-rule were once more in the ascendant. Scores of artists did as he did. London, in fact, experienced a kind of musical invasion. 'Walking in Regent Street, or Bond Street, or, more particularly, in the neighbourhood of Leicester Square,' says Wilhelm Kuhe, 'one might, without any stretch of imagination, have imagined oneself in Paris.' Chopin was only one of a great company of invaders—a company which included Kalkbrenner, Thalberg, Berlioz, Ernst, Schulhoff and Charles Hallé. Hallé explains the situation so well to his parents in a letter he wrote from London in April that I cannot do better than quote him:

Paris is in a sad and pitiable state, and God knows if it will ever recover itself; that my position there, at least for the present, is quite lost, you will already have guessed. All my colleagues are in the same case. I have been here in London three weeks, striving hard to make a new position, and I hope I shall succeed; pupils I already have, although as yet they are not many. The competition is very keen, for, beside the native musicians, there are at present here Thalberg, Chopin, Kalkbrenner, Pixis, Osborne, Prudent, Pillet and a lot of other pianists beside myself, who have all, through necessity, been driven to England, and we shall probably end by devouring one another. . . . O damnable Revolution!

If Chopin had not considered it bad form to swear, he too might have exclaimed: 'O damnable Revolution!'

CHAPTER VIII

ENGLAND AND SCOTLAND

CHOPIN arrived in London on his second visit on 21st April 1848—curiously enough, the identical day and month of Mendelssohn's first arrival in 1829. His first lodging was at 10 Bentinck Street, but in a few days he removed to 48 Dover Street, two doors from Piccadilly. 'Here I am just settled,' he wrote to Franchomme on 1st May. 'I have at last a room —fine and large—where I shall be able to breathe and play, and the sun visits me to-day for the first time. I feel less suffocated this morning, but all last week I was good for nothing.' Chopin did not love our 'province in brick,' as Madame de Staël called the English metropolis. Mendelssohn—amidst the glories of a Naples spring, too!—could write of London: 'My heart swells when I even think of the smoky nest, fated now and ever to be my favourite residence.' Chopin would rather be 'where falls not hail, nor rain, nor any snow'; in 'bowery hollows crowned with summer sea.' All through this visit he found the want of sunshine depressing.

But Chopin had little time to think of the weather. His rooms were crowded with visitors; he had three pianos: a Broadwood, a Pleyel and an Erard, and his days 'passed like lightning.' The Duchess of Sutherland presented him to the queen, and the *élite* of London society flocked round him. Lady Blessington dragged him to Gore House, the well-known rendezvous of a distinguished literary and artistic circle, and made him play there. He played also at the

114

Duchess of Sutherland's. Macready arranged a dinner in his honour, at which he was to have met Thackeray, Berlioz, Mrs. Procter, Sir Julius Benedict and other notabilities; but he was unable to be present. He was introduced to Jenny Lind (who sent him 'an excellent "stall" for the Opera'), and liked her exceedingly, perhaps because she sided with him in the George Sand affair. 'What a Swedish character!' he exclaimed. Twice he was tempted to play at a public *matinée*, first at the house of his friend Mrs. Sartoris (*née* Adelaide Kemble), and secondly at the house of Lord Falmouth. The *Times* advertisement of the latter concert runs:

Monsieur Chopin begs to announce that his second *Matinée Musicale* will take place on Friday next, 7th July, at the residence of Lord Falmouth, No. 2 St. James's Square. To commence at half-past three. Tickets, limited in number, and full particulars at Cramer, Beale & Co.'s, 201 Regent Street.

For the Sartorises' *matinée* the tickets were priced at a guinea each, and about a hundred and fifty people were present. The most interesting notices of both *matinées* are those of Henry Chorley in the *Athenæum*. 'After the hammer and tongs work on the pianoforte, to which we have of late years been accustomed,' says this discerning critic, 'the delicacy of M. Chopin's tone and the elasticity of his passages are delicious to the ear.' Novelties of fingering are noted; the player's 'peculiar mode of treating the scale and the shake'; and, of course, the much-discussed *tempo rubato*. Berlioz declared that Chopin could not keep time. Chorley says that in music not his own he 'can be as staid as a metronome.' His own compositions he plays with 'a certain freak and licence; leaning about within his bars more than any player we recollect; but still subject to a presiding sentiment of measure.'

This admirable criticism may be recalled later on when we come to deal with Chopin as a player.

All the accounts of these London appearances dwell on the composer's physically wretched state. At Lord Falmouth's, says one writer, he 'came into the room bent double, and with a distressing cough. He looked like a revived corpse. It seemed almost impossible that such an emaciated-looking man had the physique to play; but when he sat down to the instrument he played with extraordinary strength and animation.' Wilhelm Kuhe, who heard him at the Sartorises' *matinée,* describes his figure as being attenuated to such a degree that he seemed to be almost transparent (George Sand used to call him *mon cher cadavre*), adding that at a party given at Chorley's he had to be carried upstairs, being too feeble to walk. At Broadwood's the same means of getting him up to the piano showroom had to be adopted. The late Charles K. Salaman, who was also at one of the *matinées,* described him as little more than a shadow of his former self and remarked especially his 'long attenuated fingers.' It saddens one to think of his miserable condition at this time, and that he was himself sad goes without saying. 'A real joy I have not felt for a long time,' he tells Gryzmala. 'I feel nothing at all: I only vegetate, waiting patiently for the end.'

To what extent Chopin's compositions were known in England at this date we cannot definitely determine. Shortly before his arrival there had appeared *An Essay on the Works of Frederic Chopin,* in which the author spoke enthusiastically of the 'original genius, untrammelled by conventionalities, unfettered by pedantry, . . . the outpourings of an unworldly and trustful soul.' But this does not mean much one way or the other. The late A. J. Hipkins wrote: 'Chopin came here [to Broadwood's] very frequently, and his playing and his compositions, *then almost unknown,* fascinated me. He played to Mr. Frederick Beale, the publisher, his Waltzes in D flat major and C sharp minor (Op. 64), now so popular, which would have been an absurd idea at that period.' Chopin's works had been published in London by Wessel, the predecessors of Messrs. Ashdown & Parry, but the sale was by no means large. 'Scarcely anybody played Chopin's music in England sixty years ago,' says Edwin Ashdown in the *Musical Herald* of April 1903.

Frederick Stapleton, Wessel's partner, was not particularly musical, but he heard Chopin play in Paris, and the performance had an extraordinary effect upon him. He felt sure that there was a fortune in publishing such music, and he persuaded Wessel to buy everything that he could of Chopin's. Few people could play it at the time, and the firm had rather a long experience of the unpopularity of Chopin. They decided to take no more of his music. Cramer published the next composition.

This is significant enough. Chopin, we may safely conclude, was then known to only a very limited number of English music-lovers. Certainly his compositions were seldom taught. Teachers in those days, in selecting pieces for their pupils, limited themselves to standard classical works. Amateurs of the better sort played Heller, while ordinary strummers and their instructors contented themselves for the most part with variations ('aggravations,' as the wits used to call them) on favourite airs and ditties. Chopin's day was not yet.

Returning from this digression, we have now to deal with the visit to Scotland. We hear first of that part of the programme in a letter to Gryzmala:

Next week I go to Lord Torphiken [*sic*], the brother-in-law of my Scottish friends, the Misses Stirling. He wrote to me and invited me heartily, as did also Lady Murray, an influential lady of high rank there, who takes an extraordinary interest in music, not to mention the many invitations I have received from various parts of England. But I cannot wander about from one place to another like a strolling musician; such a vagabond life is hateful to me, and not conducive to my health. I intend to remain in Scotland till 29th August, on which day I go as far as Manchester, where I am engaged to play in public. I shall play there twice without orchestra, and receive for this sixty pounds.

Chopin evidently started for Scotland early in August, for on the sixth of the month he writes to Franchomme from Calder House, the residence of Lord Torpichen, some twelve miles from Edinburgh. He says his health is not 'altogether bad,' but adds that he has 'become more feeble,' and that the air of the north does not yet agree with him. The people, however, are good, though he says they are ugly; and there are 'charming, mischievous - looking cattle, perfect milk, butter, eggs, and *tout ce qui en suit*, cheese and chickens' to compensate for the ugliness! The park is very beautiful, with hundred-year-old trees; the lord of the manor very excellent. Above his private apartment (he notes this himself, though it seems odd enough), John Knox dispensed for the first time the Sacrament.[1] He has a Broadwood piano in his room, and Miss Stirling's Pleyel in his *salon*. He has paper and pens, too, in plenty, and a 'perfect tranquillity,' but he does not find one musical idea in his head. He is out of his groove, like an ass at a masked ball, or the highest string of a violin on a double bass. And he desires so much to compose a little, 'were it only to please these good ladies, Mme Erskine and Mlle Stirling.'

About these 'good ladies' it is necessary to say something

[1] This is the subject of an unfinished painting by Sir David Wilkie in the Scottish National Gallery.

CALDER HOUSE, MIDLOTHIAN

before going further. Lord Torpichen, we have already learned from Chopin himself, was their brother-in-law. Both were members of a noted Scottish family, their father being John Stirling of Kippendavie, a cousin[1] of the William Stirling of Keir who in 1865 became Sir William Stirling-Maxwell. Jane Maxwell Stirling (Chopin's Mlle Stirling) was a cousin and great friend of Thomas Erskine of Linlathen, who regarded her as one of the most remarkable women he had ever met. Her sister Catherine became the wife of James Erskine in 1811, but she had been thirty-two years a widow at the date of Chopin's visit. Jane, the younger of the two sisters, had lived a good deal in Paris, and the fact seems to be established that she made Chopin's acquaintance by becoming one of his pupils. At all events, it is on record that soon after he met her he 'began to like her,' and we know that he dedicated two of his compositions to her—the Nocturnes, Op. 55, published in 1844. It was said, not unnaturally, that she was in love with the composer, and the rumour got abroad that they were to be married. One day, when Chopin was ill, he remarked to a favourite pupil: 'They have married me to Miss Stirling; she might as well marry death.'

Later on we shall see the extent of Miss Stirling's practical interest in Chopin. Meantime it is necessary to move with the composer to Edinburgh, which he now used as a centre for making a round of visits. At this time and for many years afterwards a Polish doctor named Lyszczynski was practising medicine in the Scottish capital. He seems to have known something of Chopin, for we read that he met the composer at the railway station and addressed him in Polish.

[1] Not a brother, as Niecks says.

Chopin

Chopin at first put up at an hotel, but he soon found that mode of life unbearable and calmly told Lyszczynski that he could not live without him. The doctor, who must have been a kindly soul, took his fellow-countryman to his house at 10 Warriston Crescent, turning the nursery into a bedroom and sending the children to stay temporarily with a friend. Some very interesting reminiscences of this visit were conveyed by Mrs. Lyszczynski to Professor Frederick Niecks. It appears that Chopin rose very late and in the morning had soup in his room. His hair was curled daily by his servant Daniel, a Frenchman of Irish ancestry; and his shirts, boots and other things were of the neatest. In fact, he was 'a *petit maître*, more vain in dress than any woman.' He was so weak that the doctor had always to carry him upstairs. After dinner he sat before the fire, often shivering with cold; then, all of a sudden, he would take his seat at the piano and play himself warm. He could bear neither dictation nor contradiction; if you told him to go to the fire he would go to the other end of the room where the piano stood. Mrs. Lyszczynski once declined to sing when he asked her, and he immediately flew into a passion. 'Doctor,' he said, 'would you take it amiss if I were to force your wife to do it?' The idea of a woman refusing *him* anything he seemed to regard as preposterous. Miss Stirling often visited him while he was at Warriston Crescent, and Mrs. Lyszczynski used to chaff him about her as a 'particular friend' of his, although she indicated to Professor Niecks that the lady's love was of the 'purely sisterly' order. Chopin took it all in good part, remarking that he had no particular friend among the ladies: he 'gave to all an equal share of attention.'

On 28th August he was in Manchester for his recital there. He had a good audience, and everything passed off well, although he was in extremely low spirits. His old friend, George A. Osborne, who had lived in Paris from 1830 to 1843, met him just before the concert, and Chopin implored him not to attend. 'You who have heard me so often in Paris,' he said, 'remain with those impressions. Your presence at the concert will be painful both to you and me.' Osborne, nevertheless, could not resist the temptation of being present, and the impression left upon him was just what Chopin had anticipated. 'His playing,' says Osborne, 'was too delicate to create enthusiasm, and I was truly sorry for him.'

The best notice of this concert is to be found in the *Manchester Guardian*:

Chopin's music and style of performance partake of the same leading characteristics—refinement rather than vigour—subtle elaboration rather than simple comprehensiveness in composition —an elegant rapid touch rather than a firm nervous grasp of the instrument. Both his compositions and playing appear to be the perfection of chamber music—fit to be associated with the most refined instrumental quartet and quartet playing—but wanting in breadth and obviousness of design and executive power to be effective in a large hall.

From Manchester Chopin proceeded to Glasgow for his recital there. In the *Courier* the following advertisement had been appearing:

Monsieur Chopin has the honour to announce that his *matinée musicale* will take place on Wednesday the 27th September, in the Merchant Hall, Glasgow. To commence at half-past two o'clock. Tickets, limited in number, half a guinea each, and full particulars to be had from Mr. Muir Wood, 42 Buchanan Street.

The net profits of this concert are said to have been exactly sixty pounds, a ridiculously low sum when we compare it with the earnings of latter-day virtuosi; nay, still more ridiculously low when we recall the fact that for two concerts in Glasgow sixteen years before Paganini had fourteen hundred pounds. Muir Wood, who had established a music publishing business in Edinburgh and Glasgow, said: 'I was then a comparative stranger in Glasgow, but I was told that so many private carriages had never been seen at any concert in the town. In fact, it was the county people who turned out, with a few of the *élite* of Glasgow society. Being a morning concert, the citizens were busy otherwise, and half a guinea was considered too high a sum for their wives and daughters.' The late Dr. James Hedderwick of Glasgow tells in his reminiscences that on entering the hall he found it about one-third full. It was obvious that a number of the audience were personal friends of Chopin. Dr. Hedderwick recognized the composer at once as a 'little, fragile-looking man, in pale-grey suit, including frock-coat of identical tint and texture, moving about among the company, conversing with different groups, and occasionally consulting his watch,' which seemed to be 'no bigger than an agate stone on the fore-finger of an alderman.' Whiskerless, beardless, fair of hair, and pale and thin of face, his appearance was 'interesting and conspicuous,' and when, 'after a final glance at his miniature horologe, he ascended the platform and placed himself at the instrument, he at once commanded attention.' Hedderwick says it was a drawing-room entertainment, more *piano* than *forte*, though not without occasional episodes of both strength and grandeur. It was perfectly apparent to him that Chopin was marked for an early grave.

In 1893, in the course of some inquiries on the subject, I found two survivors of that Glasgow audience of 1848. The first was Mr. Julius Seligmann, the president of the Glasgow Society of Musicians, who died in April 1903. I asked Mr. Seligmann to state in writing what he remembered, and he sent me the following:

Several weeks before the concert Chopin lived with different friends or pupils on their invitations in the surrounding counties. I think his pupil, Miss Jane Stirling, had something to do with all the general arrangements. Mr. Muir Wood managed the special arrangements of the concert, and I distinctly remember him telling me that he never had so much difficulty in arranging a concert as on this occasion. Chopin constantly changed his mind. Wood had to visit him several times at the house of Admiral Napier, at Milliken Park,[1] near Johnstone, but scarcely had he returned to Glasgow when he was summoned back to alter something. The concert was given in the Merchant Hall, Hutcheson Street, now the County Buildings, and the horses and carriages before the hall towards the close of the concert were a splendid sight. The hall was about three-quarters filled. Between Chopin's playing, Madame de Marguerite, daughter of a well-known London physician, sang, and Mr. Muir Wood accompanied her. Chopin was evidently very ill. His touch was very feeble, and while the finish, grace, elegance and delicacy of his performances were greatly admired by the audience, the want of power made his playing somewhat monotonous. I do not remember the whole programme, but he was encored for his well-known Mazurka in B flat (Op. 7, No. 1), which he repeated with quite different nuances from those of the first. The audience was very aristocratic, consisting mostly of ladies, among whom were the Duchess of Argyll and her sister, Lady Blantyre.

Death has also claimed the second enthusiastic member of that Glasgow audience of 1848 to whom I have referred—namely Mr. George Russell Alexander, son of the proprietor of the Glasgow Theatre Royal. Mr. Alexander, in a letter

[1] A mistake: Chopin was the guest of Mrs. Houston, a sister of Miss Stirling, at Johnstone Castle.

to me, remarks especially upon Chopin's pale, cadaverous appearance. 'My emotion,' he says, 'was so great that two or three times I was compelled to retire from the room to recover myself. I have heard all the best and most celebrated stars of the musical firmament, but never one has left such an impression on my mind.'

There was still, in 1903, one survivor of the Glasgow recital of 1848 in the person of a lady then resident in Bedford, a member of a well-known Scottish family, who had the privilege of receiving some lessons from Chopin when she was in Paris in 1846. I quote from her letter to me of 18th March 1903:

The lady to whom I was indebted for my introduction to Chopin was the late Miss Stirling of Kippenross, to whom he dedicated his two Nocturnes (Op. 55). During part of his stay in Scotland he was the guest of the late Mrs. Houston of Johnstone Castle, Miss Stirling's sister. I was invited, with one of my sisters, to meet him. He was then in a most suffering state, but nevertheless he was so kind as to play to us that evening in his own matchless style. We four were his only auditors. It was at such times, and not in a concert-room, that he poured himself out. The following morning, a cold, ungenial day, we accompanied him to Glasgow. I have not preserved the programme of that memorable recital, nor can I now recall distinctly anything but the marvellous brilliancy of the well-known Mazurka (Op. 7), and the equally familiar Valses (Op. 64), the second of which is so pathetic. I never saw Chopin again, but his tones still ring in my ears.

In a second letter the same correspondent writes:

It goes to my heart to think of Chopin in his miserable state handed about among those kind and well-meaning, but tormenting friends, and forced to appear in public. Even had he been in possession of his full powers, his peculiar genius could not have been understood or appreciated in this country at that time. And

I well remember one of his friends, a consummate musician in Paris, remarking that probably his music would die with him, or at least that it would not survive after those artists had gone who could play in his own spirit, and had imbibed it from himself. But the result has been quite different.

From Glasgow Chopin appears to have gone direct to the residence of the Stirlings at Keir; at any rate we find him writing from there on 1st October. That date was a Sunday, and Chopin complains that there is 'no post, no carriage (not even for taking the air), no boat, not a *dog* to be seen—all desolate, desolate.' To make matters worse, a thick mist had settled down, and nothing could be seen of what the composer calls 'the view most celebrated for its beauty in Scotland.' Chopin became more depressed than ever. Things, he says, are getting worse with him every day. He cannot compose, partly from physical reasons, and partly because he is every week in a different place. Invitations he has in plenty, and cannot go even where he would like—for instance, to the Duchess of Argyll's. 'I am all the morning,' he writes, 'unable to do anything, and when I have dressed myself I feel again so fatigued that I must rest. After dinner I must sit two hours with the gentlemen, hear what they say, and see how much they drink. Meanwhile, I feel bored to death.' When he has settled down in some measure he must continue his travels, for, as he remarks, 'my Scots ladies do not allow me—to be sure with the best intention in the world—any rest. They fetch me to introduce me to all their relations; they will at last kill me with their kindness, and I must bear it out of pure amiability.' Much of this depression was clearly due to the state of his health. Chopin was naturally fond of society, but when he had to be carried upstairs to his bedroom, there to be undressed by his 'good Daniel,' it was hardly to be expected that he would shine in the company of those who thought they were honouring him by putting such a strain on his feeble constitution.

A week after the Glasgow concert—that is to say, on 4th October—Chopin gave an evening recital in the Hopetoun Rooms, Queen Street, Edinburgh. The tickets, as at Glasgow, were half a guinea each. Miss Stirling had grave doubts as to the support of the Edinburgh public at such an unheard-of charge, and, to make sure of the hall being respectably filled, she bought up fifty pounds' worth of tickets for distribution amongst her friends. The concert, as a natural result, was attended almost solely by the nobility and the profession. Even if the charge for admission had been less than it was there would probably have been only a small audience. Chopin was practically unknown in England; he was, we may say, wholly unknown in Scotland. Miss Stirling's fears were well-founded, and, however much Chopin may have deplored her irksome attachment, she clearly proved a good friend to him while in the north. The notices of the Edinburgh concert are not without interest. The following is from the *Courant*:

Chopin's compositions have been too long before the musical portion of Europe, and have been too highly appreciated, to require any comment, further than that they are among the best specimens of classical excellence in pianoforte music. Of his execution we need say nothing further than that it is the most finished we have ever heard. He has neither the ponderosity, nor the digital power of a Mendelssohn, a Thalberg or a Liszt; consequently his execution would be less effective in a large room; but as a chamber pianist he stands unrivalled. Notwithstanding the amount of musical entertainment already offered the Edinburgh public this season, the rooms were filled with an audience who, by their judicious and well-timed applause, testified their appreciation of the high talent of Monsieur Chopin.

Chopin himself says simply: 'I have played in Edinburgh. The nobility of the neighbourhood came to hear me; people say the thing went off well—a little success and money. There were this year in Scotland Jenny Lind, Grisi, Alboni, Mario —everybody.'

By this time Chopin was impatient to be at home in Paris. The 'beautiful country of Walter Scott, with its memories of Mary Stuart,' is all very well, but the sun does 'nothing more than usual,' and the winter advances. Everywhere he had met with extreme kindness—'interminable dinners, and cellars of which I avail myself less.' But Scotland was an alien country after all, and Chopin was never cut out for a cosmopolitan. 'A day longer here and I shall go mad or die! My Scots ladies are good, but so tedious that—God have mercy on us! they have so attached themselves to me that I cannot easily get rid of them.'

Back in London, Chopin took lodgings at 4 St. James's Place. But it was merely a passing through. He played at the Guildhall, at a ball given for the benefit of the Polish refugees, on 16th November. Patriotism would not allow him to refuse this small service to his countrymen. But his part in the affair was, if well-intentioned, a huge mistake. The people who went into the room where he played, hot from dancing, were but little in the humour to pay attention to the most poetical of pianists, and were anxious to return to their amusement. Chopin was in the last stage of exhaustion; the whole thing resulted in disappointment to all concerned. The parting shot came from the other side, at Boulogne, through which he passed in January 1849 on his way to Paris. 'Do you see the cattle in that meadow?' said the composer to M. Niedzwiecki, who travelled with him. 'They have more intelligence than the English.'

CHAPTER IX

LAST DAYS

CHOPIN'S last days need not detain us long. For some years now it had been quite evident to his friends that he could not live. In 1847 his legs had begun to swell, and he was described as a painful spectacle, the picture of exhaustion; the back bent, the head bowed, but 'always amiable and full of distinction.' Another who knew him says: 'In seeing him so puny, thin and pale, one thought for a long time that he was dying, and then one got accustomed to the idea that he could always live so.' Wolff told Niecks that latterly he did not leave the carriage when he had business at Schlesinger's music-shop: he sat closely wrapped in his blue mantle, and a shopman came out to him. Sometimes there was a temporary improvement in his health—a sort of flux and reflux of life. As Heller said, to-day he was ill, to-morrow one saw him walking on the boulevards in a thin coat. Even in his worst days the usual unconquerable hope of the consumptive served as a merciful anodyne to his feelings. 'Perhaps I may get well again,' he tells Gryzmala a few months before the end. But the illusion was cruelly dispelled.

In August 1849 he writes to Woyciechowski: 'Nothing but my being so severely ill as I am should prevent me from hastening to you at Ostend. Nevertheless I trust that, by the goodness of God, you may be permitted to come to me. The doctors will not allow me to travel. I am confined to my room, and am drinking Pyrenean water, but your presence would do me more good than all these medicines.' In a still more touching letter, written on 12th September, he pleads for his friend's presence. 'I am not,' he says, 'egotistic enough to ask you to come only on my account; for, as I am ill, you would have but few weary hours and disappointments, but perhaps also hours of comfort and of beautiful reminiscences of our youth, and I wish only that our time together may be a time of happiness.' Chopin's regard for this friend of his youth was almost pathetic in its intensity. One might say that it was 'passing the love of women.' Alas! there was to be for these two no 'time together' on this side the narrow sea.

Chopin was now no longer able to take pupils regularly. The main source of his income being thus cut off, he became distracted about the state of his finances. What money he had made in England had apparently gone, or was fast going. Friends relieved him as far as they could without risk of injury to his feelings. Thus his rooms in the Rue Chaillot were represented as costing just half what they did, the other half, according to Franchomme, being paid by a Russian lady, the Countess Obreskov. Miss Stirling, again, sent him a gift of twenty-five thousand francs, hearing of his need through one of his pupils. There is more than one version of this romantic incident. Niecks says that when Madame Rubio told Miss Stirling of the composer's straitened circumstances she was quite startled, having some short time before sent him twenty-five thousand francs anonymously. The packet, so the story goes, was eventually discovered in a clock belonging to the portress of Chopin's house. The portress had forgotten—intentionally perhaps—to hand it over when first delivered, and had then kept it, fearing trouble over the delay. Madame Rubio says that Chopin retained only a thousand francs of the money; Franchomme puts the sum down at twelve thousand francs. Whatever the sum was it would be curious if Chopin's pride had not been hurt by accepting it. In money matters he was no Wagner, who regarded it as a duty of the State or the individual with the purse to keep the genius going.

About this time he sustained a heavy blow by the death of his medical adviser, Dr. Molin, in whom he had supreme confidence. 'He felt his loss keenly,' says Liszt; 'nay, it brought a profound discouragement with it. . . . He per-suaded himself that no one could replace the trusted physician, and he had no faith in any other. Dissatisfied with them all, without any hope from their skill, he changed them constantly, and a kind of superstitious depression seized him.' Count Tarnowski says he insisted on the attendance of Dr. Blache, one of the then celebrated physicians for children's illnesses. 'He will help me most,' remarked the invalid, 'as there is something of a child in me.' He moved from one lodging to another, and at last settled down to die at No. 12 Place Vendôme.

When October came he could no longer sit up without support. As Berlioz told in an obituary article, even the slightest conversation gave him terrible distress, so that he endeavoured generally to make himself understood by signs. Fortunately, he was not left to the care of strangers. His sister, Ludwika Jedrzejewicz, came with her husband and daughter from Poland, and was with him to the last. Adolf Gutmann, too, his friend and most distinguished pupil, was in constant attendance. Chopin feared that Gutmann would not be able, from fatigue, to continue his nursing. His presence, said he, 'is dearer to me than that of any other person.' The Countess Delphine Potocka, one of his warmest admirers, to whom he had dedicated the F minor Concerto, hurried from Nice to be beside him. When Chopin learned of her arrival, he implored her to sing. Liszt is picturesque over this incident. He writes:

The piano was rolled to the door of his chamber, while with sobs in her voice and tears streaming down her cheeks, his gifted countrywoman sang. She sang that famous Canticle to the Virgin which, it is said, once saved the life of Stradella. 'How beautiful it is!' he exclaimed. 'My God, how very beautiful! Again! again!' Though overwhelmed with emotion, the countess had the noble courage to comply with the last wish of a friend and compatriot: she again took a seat at the piano, and sang a hymn from Marcello. Chopin now feeling worse, everybody was seized with fright. By a spontaneous impulse all who were present threw themselves upon their knees—no one ventured to speak; the sacred silence was only broken by the voice of the singer floating like a melody from heaven above the sighs and sobs which formed its mournful earthly accompaniment.

The point is not very important, but it should be stated that there is some doubt about the countess having sung 'that famous Canticle to the Virgin.' According to Niecks, 'Gutmann positively asserted that she sang a psalm by Marcello and an air by Pergolesi, while Franchomme insisted on her having sung an air from Bellini's *Beatrice di Tenda,* and that only once, and nothing else.' Gutmann and Franchomme were both present on the occasion, Liszt was not. Clearly Liszt was mistaken. But, then, how came Gutmann and Franchomme to differ so greatly in regard to a matter which must have deeply impressed itself on their memories? M. Gavard, who was among those in attendance on Chopin towards the end, said frankly that he did not know what the countess sang. The scene had overpowered his sensibility, and he remembered 'only the moment when the death-rattle of the departing one interrupted the countess in the middle of the second piece.'

This strange conflict of evidence which presents itself so often in the career of Chopin applies also to the incident of George Sand's visit to the sick-room, to which passing reference has already been made. M. Gavard, to whose daughter Elise, by the way, the *Berceuse* is dedicated, says that George Sand sent a lady, a Madame M., to inquire about Chopin. Gutmann, on the other hand, declares that 'George Sand came herself to the landing of the staircase and desired to be allowed to see Chopin, but that he strongly advised her against such a course, deeming it liable to affect the patient disastrously.' This seems the most reasonable version of a much debated incident. Gutmann's attitude was based on grounds of common prudence, and so far is perfectly intelligible; but doubtless there was something more behind his refusal. There is always a certain jealousy around a death-bed, even when there is no prospective property to inherit. Each relative or friend imagines that he or she is the one person who can best soothe the last moments. In this case there was, further, the detestation in which many of Chopin's friends held George Sand, and their conviction, right or wrong, that she had wrecked his life. The ladies especially would have felt the death-bed polluted by the presence of one whom somebody called a *mangeuse des hommes*, and would have thought it impossible for Chopin in that atmosphere to make a noble end. And so George Sand was excluded. 'It may be that the decision was right,' says Sir Henry Hadow, 'and yet Chopin spoke of her and wondered at her absence. The fire of life is sacred in its lowest embers, yet a breath of love might have fanned them into a purer flame. In all Chopin's story there is nothing more pathetic

MARCELLINE CZARTORYSKA, NÉE PRINCESS RADZIWILL
After an Engraving by Marchi

than the narrow chasm which kept asunder two severed hearts at the very point of union.' For my part, I think that Chopin's passage into the darkness was all the easier for his being spared an interview which must have recalled old agitation and bitterness. Certainly George Sand could have done no more for him in his helpless state than was being done by the tender and devoted hands of those around him. The following from M. Gavard's recollections puts this plainly enough:

In the back room lay the poor sufferer, tormented by fits of breathlessness, and only by sitting in bed resting in the arms of a friend could he procure air for his oppressed lungs. It was Gutmann, the strongest among us, who knew best how to manage the patient, and who mostly thus supported him. At the head of his bed sat the Princess Czartoryska: she never left him, guessing his most secret wishes, nursing him like a Sister of Mercy, with a serene countenance which did not betray her deep sorrow. Other friends gave a helping hand or relieved her—every one according to his power; but most of them stayed in the two adjoining rooms. Every one had assumed a part; every one helped as much as he could: one ran to the doctor, to the apothecary; another introduced the persons asked for; a third shut the door on the intruders. To be sure, many who had anything but free entrance came, and called to take leave of him just as if he were about to start on a journey. This ante-room of the dying, where every one of us waited and watched, was like a guard-house or a camp.

The part taken by the Princess Marcelline Czartoryska in these tender ministrations is not overrated by M. Gavard. Liszt says she passed every day a couple of hours with the dying man. She 'left him at the last, only after having prayed for a long time beside him, who had just then fled from this world of illusions and sorrow.' The princess was one of Chopin's best pupils. She had been trained by Czerny before coming to him, and was a first-rate pianist.

She appeared in many charity concerts, often played with Franchomme the Sonata for cello and piano, and played also with Liszt in Vienna, when the master accompanied her on a second piano in the *largo* from Chopin's second Concerto. In 1855 she gave a recital in London at the Marquis of Breadalbane's, for the benefit of the Polish Society—tickets forty shillings each—and 'played beautifully.'[1] She died in June 1894 at her castle near Cracow.

Chopin retained consciousness almost to the last. George Sand says that the idea of his own death was associated with all the superstitious imaginings of Slavonic poetry. Latterly, however, he had been looking forward to his dissolution with comparative serenity. Once when the physician was feeling his pulse, he broke the silence with the words: 'Now my death struggle begins.' The physician sought to soothe him with some commonplace remark, but Chopin rejoined with a superiority which admitted of no reply: 'God shows man a rare favour when He reveals to him the moment of the approach of death; this grace He shows me. Do not disturb me.' Now and again a peevish complaint would escape his lips. 'Why do I suffer so?' he would ask. 'If it were in a battle I should understand it, because I could serve as an example to others. But to die so miserably on my bed—how can my suffering benefit any one?' He discussed the question of his manuscripts with his sister, and begged that all his inferior compositions should be burned. 'I owe it to the public,' he said, 'and to myself to publish only good things. I kept to this resolution all my life; I wish to keep to it now.' What a pity it is that those who had the responsible guardianship of his manuscripts did not respect his dying desire in this matter. Franchomme

[1] See an article, with portrait of the princess, in the *Magazine of Music* for June 1893.

stated that Pleyel pointedly asked him what was to be done with the manuscripts, and received for reply that they were to be distributed among his friends, that none were to be published, and that fragments were to be destroyed. It is therefore perfectly clear that his wishes were ignored, which is all the more to be regretted in that hardly any of the posthumous compositions are worthy of him at his best.

On 16th October Chopin became suddenly worse, and the Abbé Jelowicki, a distinguished Polish emigrant, was sent for, the dying composer remarking that he had not confessed for many years, and wished to do so now. After the holy Viaticum had been administered and the absolution pronounced, Chopin embraced his confessor. 'Thanks! thanks to you,' he said, 'I shall not now die like a pig.' The difficulty of respiration—the only indication, indeed, that he was still alive—had greatly increased, and that same evening two doctors examined him. They could do nothing. Death was already at the door. About two o'clock on the morning of the 17th he drank some wine held to his lips by the faithful Gutmann. Turgenev makes ironic reference to the half-hundred countesses in Europe who claimed to have held the dying Chopin in their arms. To Gutmann alone belonged the mournful distinction. 'Cher ami,' he said, and, kissing his pupil's hand, he passed into the eternal silence. In the words of Liszt, he died as he had lived—loving. It was a beautiful death, beautiful as that of Mozart, beautiful as his own music.

Mention has just been made of the Abbé Jelowicki. In the second edition of Liszt's rhapsody on the composer reference is made to a conversation which he had with the abbé regarding the last hours of Chopin, and a statement written by the abbé is quoted in Niecks's biography. A more extended reminiscence, written originally in French, was first translated and published in the *Allgemeine Musikzeitung*; and this appears, in an English translation, in James Huneker's monograph, where it fills half a dozen pages. My first impulse was to reprint it in full, but on second thoughts I decided that it was worthless. The abbé's bias towards edifi-cation is too evident. It may have been true enough that Chopin's soul was, as he says, 'dearer to me than all his talent'; but the lover of Chopin resents being told that Chopin's success as an artist checked in him 'the expression of faith and prayer'; that only the innate promptings of his better nature 'hindered him from indulging in sarcasm and mockery over holy things and the consolations of religion.' One has misread the character of Chopin entirely if this picture of a 'rebellious soul' be true.

Moreover, the abbé's account of these last few days stands so completely alone in its details that I am inclined to doubt the authenticity of the document altogether. Look at the following before we pass on:

He blessed his friends, and when, after an apparently last crisis, he saw himself surrounded by the crowd that day and night filled his chamber, he asked me: 'Why do they not pray?' At these words all fell on their knees, and even the Protestants joined in the litanies and prayers for the dying.

Day and night he held my hand, and would not let me leave him. 'No, you will not leave me at the last moment,' he said, and leaned on my breast as a little child in a moment of danger hides itself in its mother's breast.

Now he called upon Jesus and Mary, with a fervour that reached to heaven; now he kissed the crucifix in an excess of faith, hope, and love. He made the most touching utterances. 'I love God and man,' he said. 'I am happy so to die; do not weep, my sister. My friends, do not weep. I am happy. I feel that I am dying. Farewell, pray for me!'

There is not a word of all this in the reminiscences of the other friends who were gathered around the dying composer, and we know for certain that it was not the abbé's hand that Chopin held 'day and night.' On the whole, I should say that the abbé, holy man as he may have been, was romancing. He was certainly at Chopin's death-bed, but these pious embellishments must be all his own invention.

Chopin had been ailing so long and reports of his death had so often been circulated that at first the news was received with incredulity; but when at length the sad fact became apparent it was accepted with the greatest regret all over Paris, and, indeed, wherever the musician and his music were known. Every one who had come in contact with him 'felt his death as a personal sorrow: one had been honoured by his friendship, another enriched by his bounty, another gladdened by some kind word or some pleasant greeting. There was no chance acquaintance but had felt his ray of reflection from the master's life.'

As the preparations for the funeral were being arranged friends came to look at the dead artist. So many floral tributes were sent that, as Liszt said, he 'seemed to sleep in a garden of roses,' amid which the face looked beautiful and young. He lay as though he had died smiling. The funeral did not take place till 30th October, when he was buried from the Madeleine with befitting ceremonial. The *Musical World*[1] described the scene as 'one of the most imposing we ever remember to have witnessed.' About three thousand people assembled to take part in the obsequies. [The Funeral March from the B flat minor Sonata, orchestrated by Réber, was performed as an introit, and Lefébure-Wély played two of the preludes on the organ.] Mozart's *Requiem* was sung, and

[1] 10th November 1849.

for its better rendering there was an uncanonical introduction of female vocalists. Lablache, who had sung the 'Tuba mirum' from the *Requiem* at Beethoven's funeral in 1827, sang it again on this occasion. Berlioz says that Chopin had expressed a wish to have the *Requiem* sung at his funeral. Gutmann and Franchomme say he did not. M. Gavard, again, declares that he had drawn up the programme of his funeral and asked that Mozart's work should be performed. Thus do the old hopeless contradictions pursue the biographer to the end.

The great door of the Madeleine was hung with black curtains, upon which Chopin's initials were emblazoned in silver. From the church the coffin was carried all along the boulevards to the cemetery of Père Lachaise—a distance of three miles at least—the procession being joined by nearly every notable man in Paris. The pall-bearers, according to Théophile Gautier, were Meyerbeer, Delacroix, Pleyel and Franchomme; but even here, again, the authorities differ, some adding the names of Gutmann and Princes Adam and Alexander Czartoryski.[1] The Polish earth which his friends had given him on leaving Warsaw nearly nineteen years before was sprinkled on his coffin, and his heart was taken to Warsaw, where it is preserved in the Church of the Holy Cross.

Chopin was buried in evening clothes, his concert dress. Niecks, on the authority of Kwiatowski, the portrait painter, says that this was not his own wish. It is, however, a Polish custom for the dying to choose their grave clothes. Liszt remarks on the custom and adds that worldly men often chose monastic robes; that official costumes were often selected or

[1] According to Henri Bidou, Prince Adam Czartoryski and Meyerbeer led the procession; Prince Alexander Czartoryski, Delacroix, Franchomme and Gutmann were pall-bearers.—E. B.

rejected, according as pleasant or painful memories were associated with them. Of all contemporary artists Chopin gave the fewest concerts, yet he desired to be carried to the grave in the clothes he had worn on these occasions—occasions, moreover, which, in later years especially, were charged for him with repugnant memories! Genius seldom does anything in the expected way.

Lombroso, who analyses human tears and human emotions with equal facility, declares that Chopin 'in his will directed that he should be buried in a white tie, small shoes and short breeches.' This, he says, was an evidence of his insanity. The statement is worth just as much as Lombroso's other absurd assertion that Chopin 'abandoned the woman whom he tenderly loved [who was this woman?] because she offered a chair to someone else before giving the same invitation to himself.'[1] Surely no more 'specious nonsense' was ever written about any other great musician than about this poor Pole, who had the misfortune to be a consumptive and to write music which 'mainly pleases the ladies.'

Chopin's last resting-place at Père Lachaise is marked by a fine monument raised by subscription. Curiously enough, it was designed by Clésinger, the husband of Solange Dude-vant. It consists of a pedestal supporting a mourning muse with a lyre in her hand, and the inscription reads: 'Frédéric Chopin, né en Pologne à Zelazowa Wola, près de Varsovie: Fils d'un émigré français, marié à Mlle Krzyzanowska, fille d'un gentilhomme polonais.' The grave is near those of Cherubini, Boieldieu, the elder Pleyel and Grétry. Abélard and Héloïse lie not far away; and seven years later an adjacent spot received the mortal remains of Heine.

[1] Lombroso gives a vague reference to George Sand's *Histoire de ma vie* for these statements (*The Man of Genius*, chap. iii, p. 47).

CHAPTER X

CHOPIN: THE MAN

CHOPIN'S appearance has been variously described. Moscheles said expressively that he looked like his music. Berlioz told Legouvé to see Chopin, 'for he is something which you have never seen, and someone you will never forget.' Liszt makes a mistake in stating that his eyes were blue, for they were brown —'more cheerful than pensive,' adds Osborne—but otherwise his description may be accepted as correct. He says that Chopin always put him in mind of 'a convolvulus balancing its azure-hued cup upon a very slight stem, the tissue of which is so vaporous that the slightest contact wounds and tears the delicate corolla.' Proceeding to less ethereal details, he notes that Chopin was short of stature and that his limbs were slight. The 'transparent delicacy' of his complexion pleased the eye, his fair hair was soft and silky, and his nose slightly aquiline.

Much attention has been bestowed on the nose; rightly perhaps, since, as Hazlitt says, the nose is the rudder of the face, the index of the will. In the Winterhalter portrait it is described as 'too Hebraic,' while in the Graefle it is likened to 'that of a predacious bird, painfully aquiline.' But all the portraits and descriptions agree as to the aquiline outline, and we had better admit, without more ado, that the Chopin nose was, like that of the Master of the House of Usher, of 'a delicate Hebrew model.' The nostrils were finely cut, the lips thin and effeminate, the under one protruding. Georges Mathias, remarking that he remembers well his hesitating, womanish ways and his distinguished manners, says: 'I see him standing with his back to the chimney. I see his fine features, his small eyes, brilliant and transparent; his mouth, opening to show the most dazzling teeth; his smile with an inexpressible charm.' Osborne also comments on the smile, which he describes as 'good-natured.' Johnson says that every man may be judged by his laughter, but no Boswell has chronicled the laughter of Frederic Chopin. His voice was 'musical but subdued,' says Osborne. This agrees with Liszt, who speaks of the tone as 'somewhat veiled, often stifled.' A. J. Hipkins, who frequently saw him in London in 1848, said he was 'about middle height, with a pleasant face, a mass of fair, curly hair like an angel, and agreeable manners.' His thin, elastic hands have already been remarked upon: the feet were correspondingly small.

The portraits, so far as I can judge, rather fail to bring out the real Chopin, though the characteristic poetic distinction, the exquisite refinement and the noble bearing of the man are common to most of them. The Clésinger head at Père La-chaise, for which the mould was taken the day after his death, is 'mediocre and lifeless,' the Kolberg portrait in possession of the Musical Society of Warsaw rather too 'mature in expres-sion.' The Vigneron portrait of 1833 was praised by Mathias, who said it was marvellous for the exact idea it gives of Chopin, 'the graceful fall of the shoulders, the Polish look, the charm of the mouth.' The Bovy medallion, which may be seen in Breitkopf & Härtel's thematic catalogue of Chopin's works, is said by the same authority to afford a very good idea of 'the outlines of his hair and nose.' The Duval portrait in Kara-sowski's biography is rightly described by Mathias as giving the composer a stupid look. There is a pencil sketch by Kwiatowski, who portrayed Chopin frequently and in many ways, of which M. Gavard says: 'This picture of Chopin is the one I like best.' The portrait by Winterhalter, dated 1847, is given in Sir Henry Hadow's work,[1] as well as the Graefle (dated 19th October 1849), which represents the dead Chopin and is somewhat ghastly. The Delacroix portrait in the Louvre[2] is a powerful piece of work, but unfortunately it represents the later Chopin, ailing and broken by suffering, the look dreamy and melancholy, the attenuated and lengthened fingers strongly accentuated. Mention has been made of the burning of a portrait by Ary Scheffer. Happily this portrait had been previously copied. There is a very good reproduction of it in the German edition of Chopin's works published by Fontana. It represents him in 'a nonchalant attitude, gentleman-like in the highest degree—the forehead superb, the hands of a rare distinction, the eyes small, the nose prominent, but the mouth of an exquisite fineness, and gently closed.' A lady pupil of Chopin said that it had the appearance of a ghost and was more pale and worn than Chopin himself. This by no means exhausts the list of portraits, though it takes account of all the more important representations. A portrait of the composer at the age of seventeen was given in the Warsaw *Echo Muzyczne* of October 1899. I have not seen it, but James Huneker describes it as 'that of a thoughtful, poetic, but not handsome lad, his hair waving over a fine forehead, a feminine mouth, large, aquiline nose, and about his slender neck a Byronic collar.'

Chopin's love of fine clothes has been noted. A hasty

---

[1] *Studies in Modern Music,* vol. ii.

[2] See frontispiece.

philosopher once observed that all men who wear velvet coats are atheists. Chopin wore at least a velvet waistcoat; like Stevenson, he may have worn a velvet coat too on occasion. One letter addressed to Fontana asks that fond disciple to 'go to my tailor and order him to make me at once a pair of grey trousers, something respectable, not striped, but plain and elastic. Also a quiet black velvet waistcoat, with very little and no loud pattern—something very quiet but very elegant.'

Chopin must always be 'very elegant.' Like Wagner with his famous dressing-gowns, he spent a great deal on his clothes, and was 'very correct in the matter of studs, walking-sticks and cravats.' Hipkins describes him as 'something of a dandy, who always wore patent leather boots and light kid gloves, and who was very particular about the cut and colour of his clothes.' Some writers have thought it necessary to apologize for him on the score of his dandyism; indeed, there is a sort of superstitious belief that genius is wanting to itself unless it goes dishevelled and down-at-heel. But a dandy is at least less offensive to his neighbours than a sloven; and while much excellent and powerful work has come out of the squalor of Grub Street, it by no means follows that a manuscript has additional value because it is stained with beer. It is at any rate a noteworthy fact that bravery of dress has often accompanied bravery in action; as Sir Henry Hadow has said, the dandies have played their part in history. Claverhouse, Lovelace, Sir Philip Sidney were all dandies, and there is nothing to surprise us if in art also a certain daintiness of taste in form and colour is associated, as it was in Chopin's case, with a certain delicacy of workmanship.

With all his dandyism, too, Chopin had an air of aristocratic bearing, a tone of high breeding, which marked him out even in the most distinguished company, and always led to his being treated, as it were, *en prince*. There was nothing hail-fellow-well-met about him. With the ordinary rank-and-file musician he could never have been popular. In Mathias's words, he was 'crazy about the aristocracy,' and he was himself an aristocrat, with all his finickiness about fine clothes and white hands and rosy finger-nails.

His dainty taste in dress extended itself in other directions. He must have his rooms artistically and expensively furnished —'something splendid,' in fact, as he tells Fontana, when that long-suffering friend is sent in search of a new habitation. There is to be 'no smoke nor bad smells, but a fine view and large garden,' and—no blacksmith in the neighbourhood! He discusses details about curtains and couches and drawing-room furniture with all the zest of a young bride. Just before he left London in 1849 he wrote to Gryzmala about the preparation of his rooms. 'Please see that some violets be bought,' he says, 'so that there may be a nice fragrance in the room. I should like also,' he adds, 'to find some books of poetry in my bedroom, as I shall in all probability be confined therein for some time.'

This love of flowers is referred to by several of his friends. Someone has remarked that a man who truly loves flowers cannot be a bad man. The remark would certainly apply to Chopin. The purity of his life and character has never been called in question. He shrank from coarseness of all sorts as a child would shrink from the embrace of an ogre. The dissipations of the 'average sensual man' not only had no fascination for him, but were actually the object of a deep-rooted disgust. It is told somewhere how he resented the visit of Liszt and a 'companion' to his rooms when he was absent. Liszt himself testifies to the high tone of his life.

CHOPIN

Anonymous Lithograph after the lost Portrait by Ary Scheffer

Speaking of his occasional bursts of gaiety, he says it was all the more piquant because he 'always kept it within the limits of perfect good taste, and held at a suspicious distance everything that could wound the most fastidious delicacy.' He was 'never known, even in moments of the greatest familiarity, to make use of an inelegant word, and improper merriment or coarse jesting would have been repulsive to him.'

The general effeminacy of his character was remarked upon by all who knew him intimately, and is insisted upon by most of his biographers. He was undoubtedly effeminate. He loved the society of women, and his letters to male friends, especially to Woyciechowski, read almost like the letters of a lover to his mistress. 'You do not require my portrait,' he writes; 'I am always with you and shall never forget you to the end of my life.' And again: 'You have no idea how much I love you. What would I not give to embrace you once more?' Niecks is sarcastic over the amount of osculation he would bestow on the intimates of his own sex. It certainly sounds curious according to John Bull notions, but John Bull cannot quite understand the 'velvety tenderness' of a nature like that of Chopin. The Gargantuan feasts of Henry Fielding's heroes are more appreciable to the British sense than the idea of an artist who lives, like the fabled chameleon, on air, or, like the fabled Paderewski, on cigarettes and seltzer. Chopin's effeminacy was in part constitutional, in part the natural outcome of the coddling and the flattery which were bestowed on him all through his career.

I have never been quite able to convince myself that Chopin did not lose something by his close contact with society. Hobnobbing with countesses in an atmosphere heavy with honeyed words and the perfume of roses and violets must have an enervating effect on the virility of any man, and when the man has only the small measure of virility with which Chopin had been endowed, the tendency must be to 'drug his talent into forgetfulness of loftier aims.'

Nevertheless, to speculate on what might have been the effect on Chopin's character and work if his circumstances had been different—if, for instance, he had had to endure Wagner's early struggles—is as profitless as to inquire what the fate of Europe might have been if the Battle of Hastings or the Battle of Waterloo had ended differently. Things *are* —we cannot alter them; and, without subscribing to the easy doctrine that whatever is is right, we may spare ourselves the useless pain of bemoaning what could never have been otherwise. Chopin went the way his temperament bore him, and his music is the expression of that temperament, with its curious mingling of buoyancy and morbidity. No battling with the storms of fate would ever have made a Beethoven of him.

Closely connected with his effeminacy were his alternating moods of exaltation and depression, his gaiety of spirits, and his deep-dyed melancholy. The tone of his letters is perpetually changing. On the same day he writes to one in the highest state of exhilaration, to another as if he found grief a positive luxury of existence. In his light-hearted moments he would 'gossip, chatter, imitate every one, cut up all manner of tricks, and, like Wagner, stand on his head.' But this gaiety was feverish. The real man was the moody, melancholy, morbidly sensitive Pole, who described himself as 'in this world like the E string of a violin on a double bass.' Chopin was, like many other geniuses, a bundle of contradictions. You could as little get hold of him, said Louis Enault, as of the scaly back of a mermaid. Kind, generous and forbearing, he could yet rate his friends as 'pigs' and 'Jews' when they failed him in any of the least of the menial services he so often demanded of them. Punctual and precise in his habits, he was halting and irresolute to the point of imbecility—an 'undecided being,' as he called himself. Playful and even coquettish at times, there was about him a certain primness and asperity which kept the average man at a distance. Simple and open as a child, fond too of children, he nevertheless showed himself somewhat of a *poseur,* as when he grew a little whisker on one side of his face, the side he turned towards his audiences. A man of education and culture, he was yet influenced by the most absurd superstitions. George Sand said of him in Majorca that he lived under a nightmare of legends. He had a horror of the numbers seven and thirteen, and, like Rossini, would never invite more than twelve guests to dinner. On no account would he undertake anything of importance on a Monday or a Friday, those days being considered unlucky in Poland. In this respect he was to the Philistines what the Gospel was to the Greeks—foolishness. George Sand says of him that 'he had no hatreds'; Liszt, that he could forgive in the noblest manner. But he could only half forgive. As Sir Henry Hadow phrases it, he lacked that broad, humane sense of pardon which obliterates a footprint upon the shore. If he once felt himself wounded he could wish no ill to his adversary, but the scar remained.

In money matters he was very particular, more, we may be sure, from necessity than from choice. 'I am a revolutionary and don't care for money,' he wrote in 1832. But the baker, the butcher and the candlestick-maker have to be paid, and Chopin had no other means of paying them than by the exercise of his art. For that reason he was exacting with the publishers. 'Pay, thou beast,' was his motto in dealing with these tradesmen. And why not? As Johnson remarked, nobody but a blockhead ever wrote except for money. Beethoven was keen in his financial transactions. 'The artist,' he said, 'deserves to be honourably remunerated.' Chopin did not love the haggling in the market-place, but it was necessary. The twenty francs a lesson which he took from his pupils did not suffice for his fastidious, extravagant tastes, and the publishers had to make up the balance. The sums they paid him look small enough now in the light of his fame, but considering the limited sale of his compositions during his lifetime they were sufficiently generous. One thing is to be noted to his credit. He would not make money out of works which he deemed beneath his own standard. Much as he detested playing in public he would yet face the crowd and take their coin rather than run to the publisher with what was unworthy of his powers. That he might have done better with his earnings is true enough. He was a bad manager—or rather no manager at all—and spent his money lavishly when he had it. But at least he never spent it in the pursuit of gross pleasures.

Of his musical preferences some indications have been given. Like Rubinstein—who by the way put Chopin fourth among his favourite composers—he put Bach decidedly first. Then came Mozart. 'You will play in memory of me and I shall hear you from beyond,' he is reported to have said to the Countess Czartoryska on his death-bed. Franchomme, thinking it would please him, replied: 'Yes, master; we will play your Sonata,' meaning the Sonata for piano and cello. 'Oh no, not mine,' said the dying composer; 'play really good music—Mozart, for instance.' Liszt says that Mozart was his ideal type, the poet *par excellence,* and this because he was always beautiful and never commonplace. Mozart's father was once present at a performance of *Idomeneo,* and afterwards reproached his son in the words: 'You are wrong in putting in it nothing for the long-eared ones.' It was precisely for such omissions that Mozart was admired by Chopin. He did not care much for Schubert, whom he found rough. It was of him that he once remarked: 'The sublime is desecrated when it is succeeded by the trivial.' One can easily understand how the rollicking fun and the sometimes 'vulgar though powerful energy' of Schubert would be abhorrent to the dreamiest and most poetical of all composers. And yet how much of Schubert is intensely pathetic. Weber's piano music he thought too operatic; Schumann's, as we have learned, he dismissed with airy contempt. Beethoven roused his enthusiasm only in the C sharp minor and certain other sonatas. Hummel he read and re-read with the greatest pleasure. Liszt he admired as a virtuoso but not as a composer, which is conceivable enough, seeing that he knew only the earlier works of that amazing personality. Neither Meyerbeer nor Berlioz was greatly to his liking. Once when talking to Gutmann about Berlioz he took up a pen, bent back the point and then let it rebound, saying: 'This is the way Berlioz composes—he sputters the ink over the pages of ruled paper and the result is as chance wills it.'

Regarding his literary tastes only a few words are necessary. They were in no way remarkable. Mathias declared that he read rarely—little except Polish poets like Mickiewicz, a volume of whose works Mathias always saw on his table. He seems indeed to have confined himself almost exclusively to Polish authors, though he certainly read Voltaire, whose *Dictionnaire philosophique* was one of the consolations of his last illness. One wonders if he read George Sand! Victor Hugo he regarded as 'too coarse and violent.' He loved Shakespeare, but, as Liszt is careful to add, 'subject to many reservations.' He thought that Shakespeare's characters were drawn too closely to life, and that their language had in it too much of truth. Evidently he would have agreed with Swift that in order to be happy it is necessary to be perpetually deceived. In literature everything that approached the melo‑dramatic gave him pain. The frantic and despairing aspects of exaggerated romanticism repelled him, and he could not endure the struggle for wondrous effects or delicious excesses. With regard to his linguistic accomplishments, he spoke French, with a Polish accent, and also German. Liszt says he did not like French: he thought it was not sufficiently sonorous, and he deemed its genius cold. Poles commonly hold this opinion.

As a letter‑writer Chopin was without distinction. We prize the letters of Mendelssohn and Berlioz, but Chopin's letters do not show any real literary quality. Some are, indeed, surprisingly slipshod. They prove that he had considerable humour, sometimes of an unexpectedly downright kind, if little wit. His little touches of malicious sarcasm and irony are enjoyable, but there is much romantic, incoherent nonsense in his epistles at which the average healthy individual can only smile. Probably it was the outlet for what of his sentimentalism he found himself unable to 'tell his piano.' Latterly he hated letter‑writing and would walk miles to answer in person a letter which in five minutes he might have answered with the pen. So at any rate says Liszt, who declares that the great majority of his friends had never seen his fine microscopic handwriting. He was certainly a bad correspondent, with 'odd fits of intermission and reticence'; and one finds it somewhat difficult to credit the recent announcement that 512 hitherto unpublished letters from his pen have been found in the hands of a niece. I should doubt very much if

Chopin wrote five hundred letters during his whole career, apart from those written to his parents.[1]

Liszt says that when he did write it was mostly to his compatriots, and that because he could address them in his native tongue. This brings one to the question of Chopin's love of country. It has been said that his patriotism was that of a woman, that the fate of Poland never touched him to any poignancy of emotion. It is not easy to determine how far this is true or untrue. He certainly loved the land of his birth, and we know that in Paris he often assisted the necessitous Poles. His more intimate friends were fellow-countrymen, and among his pupils he showed a distinct preference for Poles. The course taken by his genius, too, suggests that Poland was very near his heart. In one place Liszt says he took no delight in the expression of patriotic feeling; in another he says that Chopin never regarded France as his country, 'as he remained faithful in his devoted affection to the eternal widowhood of his own.' Orlowski wrote of him from Paris in 1834 that 'the yearning after his country consumes him.' But this is an obvious exaggeration. Chopin was to all intents and purposes a Parisian, living on and nourished by the gaieties of the best circles in Parisian society. It seems in the last degree unlikely that one who thus fed on the smiles and slavish adulation of aristocratic ladies, basking in boudoirs and *salons,* would suffer keenly on the score of his country's wrongs. Too much has been made of the alleged reflection of this patriotic spirit in his music. In the great bulk of his compositions there is comparatively little of which one can say with absolute confidence that it gives expression to a passionate protest in favour of Poland. Much in Beethoven is

[1] The Opienski collection, published in English in 1932, contains 294 letters.—E. B.

tinged with a kindred sadness and gloom, and yet Beethoven had nothing to complain of about the fate of his fatherland.

Of Chopin's religion it is possible to say little more than that he was reared in the Roman Catholic Church, and that he died, as we have seen, confessing her faith. 'In order not to offend my mother,' he remarked to the Abbé Jelowicki, 'I would not die without the sacraments, but for my part I do not regard them in the sense that you desire.' Liszt says he was 'sincerely religious,' but that he held his faith without calling attention to it, and never touched upon the subject. 'It was possible to be acquainted with him a long time without knowing what were his religious views.' In this he was refreshingly like the normal sensible man, who shrinks from being too closely catechized.

CHAPTER XI

CHOPIN: THE TEACHER AND PLAYER

'CAN you fancy this Ariel of the piano giving lessons to humdrum pupils? Playing in a charmed and bewitching circle of countesses, surrounded by the luxury and the praise that kills, Chopin is a much more natural figure.' So writes an American biographer. The question inevitably suggests itself. Yet Chopin gave lessons regularly, and what is more, appeared, unlike Schubert, to relish giving them. He taught for at least eight months of the year, and was always fully occupied. His pupils adored him. His kindness and his patience were generally remarked, and when a pupil gave indication of talent his interest and attention were doubled. Carl Mikuli, one of his pupils, says: 'Chopin made great demands on the talent and diligence of the pupil. A holy, artistic zeal burned in him; every word was incentive and inspiring. . . . Single lessons often lasted literally for hours at a stretch.'

He would have been more than human if he had not occasionally lost his temper, but he 'always softened at once if the culprit showed any symptoms of distress.' Another of his pupils, Georges Mathias, says that when he was pleased he would remark: 'Very well, my angel.' When he was not pleased he would tear his hair, disagreeable words and sheets of music would fly in the air, and that small delicate feminine hand would break lead pencils like reeds. Mathias once saw him break a chair in his despairing rage at some incompetent player. He adds that in giving a lesson Chopin 'became a poet.' Thus at a certain place in Weber's A flat major Sonata he would whisper: 'An angel passed into heaven.'

From other pupils we gather many interesting details as to the qualities upon which he insisted, about his method of dealing with technique, and about the composers he favoured most. Every pupil, however accomplished, had to begin with Clementi's *Gradus* and to take the usual course of studies and exercises. His great object was to get the left hand perfectly independent, so that it might keep the time regularly, whilst the right was more free to develop the theme under treatment. His system of fingering was in a manner an outcome of the requirements of his own music. The old dictum, according to which the thumb and fourth finger were never to be used on the black keys except in very rare cases, had no place in his code of rules. He frequently passed the thumb after the third or fourth finger, and in ascending passages the second and third fingers over the fourth. No doubt, as Hans von Bülow remarks, this peculiar fingering was to some extent traceable to his favourite Pleyel piano. Before Pleyel adopted the double escapement he certainly produced instruments with the most pliant touch possible, and on these instruments Chopin would regard the use of the thumb in the ascending scale on two white keys in succession as thoroughly practicable. On the grand piano of the present day we, of course, regard this as irreconcilable with conditions of *legato* and *crescendo*.

With Chopin a sympathetic touch was the first essential for a pianist. 'Is that a dog barking?' he would say when a pupil played roughly. In order to get this sympathetic touch he insisted upon an easy position of the hand. He required the fingers of the right hand to be so placed that they should rest on the notes E, F sharp, G sharp, A sharp and B; those of the left on C, B flat, A flat, G flat and E. As Charles Willeby points out, if the fingers are placed in this way it will be found that the hands are somewhat turned in opposite directions, and are more ready for the rapid execution of scale passages and arpeggios than in any other position. When teaching a pupil Chopin adhered strictly to this. He would even submit temporarily to the uneven execution of some passages until the player became used to his position of the hands. He demanded that the hand should be held absolutely flat. He advised all his pupils to learn singing in order to acquire a fine tone. 'Listen carefully and often to great singers,' he would tell them. He hated affectation and all exaggerated accents. 'Play as you feel,' he would often say. Which is not always, it may be added, a safe rule.

We get some hints of all this in a fragmentary *Méthode des Méthodes,* the manuscript of which was given to the Princess M. Czartoryska by his sister after his death.[1] He says here that in learning the scales it is unnecessary to begin with that of C major, which is the easiest to read but *the most difficult to play,* as it lacks the support afforded by the black notes. He would take, first of all, the scale of G flat major, 'which places the hand regularly, utilizing the long fingers for the black keys.' From this he would work back to the scale of C, using each time one finger less on the black keys. The shake should be played with three fingers, or with four as an exercise. The chromatic scale should be practised with the thumb, the forefinger, and the middle finger; also with the little finger,

[1] A translation of this manuscript appears in Natalie Janotha's edition of Jan Kleczynski's *Chopin's Greater Works* (London, 1896). Liszt makes a mistake in saying that the fragment was destroyed.

the third, and the middle fingers. In thirds, as in sixths and octaves, the same fingers should always be used. Then the composer goes on to say that no one notices inequality in the power of the notes of a scale when it is played very fast and equally as regards time. In a good mechanism the aim is, not to play everything with an equal tone, but to acquire a beautiful quality of sound and a perfect shading. For a long time players have acted against nature in seeking to give an equal power to each finger. On the contrary, each finger should have an appropriate part assigned to it. The thumb has the greatest power, being the thickest finger and the freest. Then comes the little finger. The middle finger is the main support of the hand, and is assisted by the first. Finally comes the third, the weakest one. As to this Siamese twin of the middle finger—bound by one and the same ligament—some players try to force it with all their might to become independent—a thing impossible and most likely unnecessary. There are many different qualities of sound, just as there are several fingers. The point is to utilize the differences, and this, in other words, is the art of fingering.

Such, in brief, is Chopin's method. It is interesting, of course, but is it practical? Is it possible to build upon it a technique such as is required of the modern virtuoso? One can only judge by results. Every teacher has his own methods, and I do not suppose that what is peculiar in Chopin's is, in these later days, allowed a chance of demonstrating either its utility or its efficacy.

I have said that we get many interesting details of Chopin as a teacher from his pupils. It is my privilege to print for the first time the following from a lady (I have already drawn upon her reminiscences in Chapter VIII) who had lessons from the master in Paris in 1846. The writer desired to remain anonymous, but I am allowed to say that she was a distant cousin of the Miss Stirling who showed her regard for Chopin in the practical way already mentioned. My correspondent's letter is dated 27th March 1903, and runs as follows:

In compliance with your request that I should tell you something about Chopin as a teacher, I can only speak from my own experience, and after the lapse of fifty-seven years my memory is naturally rather hazy, though I can recall some incidents distinctly.

My first interview with Chopin took place at his rooms in Paris. Miss Jane Stirling had kindly arranged that my sister and I should go with her. I remember the bright fire in his elegant and comfortable *salon*. It was in this very month of March, 1846. In the centre of the room stood two pianofortes—one grand, the other upright. Both were Pleyels, and the tone and touch most beautiful.

In a few moments Chopin entered from another room and received us with the courtesy and ease of a man accustomed to the best society. His personal appearance, his extreme fragility and delicate health have been described again and again, and also the peculiar charm of his manner. Miss Stirling introduced me as her *petite cousine* who was desirous of the honour of studying with him. He was very polite, but did not give a decided assent at once. Finally he fixed a day and hour for my first lesson, requesting me to bring something I was learning. I took Beethoven's Sonata in A flat (Op. 26). I need hardly say I felt no slight trepidation on taking my place at the grand piano, Chopin seated beside me. I had not played many bars before he said: 'Laissez tomber les mains.' Hitherto I had been accustomed to hear: 'Put down your hands,' or 'Strike' such a note. This *letting fall* was not mechanical only: it was to me a new idea, and in a moment I felt the difference. Chopin allowed me to finish the beautiful air, and then took my place and played the entire sonata. It was like a revelation. You are doubtless well acquainted with the celebrated *Marche funèbre* which of late has so often been played on mournful occasions in public, in conjunction with Chopin's own most beautiful and pathetic composition. He played that *Marche funèbre* of Beethoven's with a grand, orchestral, powerfully dramatic effect, yet with a sort of restrained emotion which was indescribable. Lastly he rushed through the final movement with faultless precision and extra-ordinary delicacy—not a single note lost, and with marvellous phrasing and alternations of light and shade. We stood spellbound, never having heard the like.

My next lesson began with the sonata. He called my attention to its structure, to the intentions of the composer throughout; showing me the great variety of touch and treatment demanded: many other points, too, which I cannot put into words. From the sonata he passed to his own compositions. These I found fascinating in the highest degree, but very difficult. He would sit patiently while I tried to thread my way through mazes of intricate and unaccustomed modulations, which I could never have under-stood had he not invariably played to me each composition—nocturne, prelude, impromptu, whatever it was—letting me hear the frame-work (if I may so express it) around which these beautiful and strange harmonies were grouped, and in addition showing me the special fingering, on which so much depended, and about which he was very strict.

He spoke very little during the lessons. If I was at a loss to understand a passage, he played it slowly to me. I often wondered at his patience, for it must have been torture to listen to my bungling, but he never uttered an impatient word. Sometimes he went to the other piano and murmured an exquisite impromptu accompani-ment. Once or twice he was obliged to withdraw to the other end of the room when a frightful fit of coughing came on, but he made signs to me to go on and take no notice.

On two occasions I arrived just at the termination of a lesson. A lady, young and very attractive, was rising from the piano. She thanked Chopin gracefully for the pleasure he had given her. She was a Russian lady of rank. On the other occasion a German lady, a professional musician, and her husband were taking leave and were expressing their obligations. I heard her say that since receiving Chopin's assistance, her studies were no longer a toil but a delight.

In sending you these fragmentary recollections, I feel it would be unfair to Chopin if they were to convey the impression that he had a cut-and-dried 'method.' The majority of his pupils, I always understood, were already excellent and even distinguished musicians before they went to him. They required no elementary teaching, whereas I was but a young amateur with only a great natural love for music and very little previous training. Chopin questioned me as to this, and I told him I had learned more from listening to singing than anything else. He remarked: 'That is right; music ought to be song.' And truly in his hands the piano *did* sing, and in many tones. I watched, I listened, but can find no adequate description of that thrilling music. One never thought of 'execution,' though that was marvellous. It seemed to come from the depths of a heart, and it struck the hearts of listeners. Volumes have been written, yet I think no one who did not hear him could quite understand that magnetic power. It is still a deep, though somewhat mournful pleasure to me to open the pages marked with Chopin's pencillings on the margins—graceful little additions to the printed music.

Although there is not much technical detail in this interesting letter it seems to realize for us Chopin the teacher much better than certain of the reminiscences of his more famous pupils. That touch about the 'frightful fit of coughing' appears to me to be particularly pathetic.

As to the compositions which Chopin used most in teaching, it is generally understood that, in addition to his own works, his pupils had to study Bach and Mozart first of all. Handel, Dussek, Beethoven, Field, Hummel, Weber and Hiller were also among his favourites. Liszt he does not seem to have taught. When he had himself to play in public he generally shut himself up for a fortnight and played nothing but Bach. He never played his own works by way of preparation.

It has been remarked as curious that none of Chopin's pupils attained anything like real distinction. Gutmann was highly considered by those who heard him, but the great world of music knew him no more than it knew Mathias, Lysberg, Mikuli, Tellefsen and others who underwent a long course of study with him. A very gifted pupil, a Hungarian named Carl Filtsch, was cut off while yet in his teens. It was of Filtsch that Liszt remarked: 'When he starts playing, I shall shut up shop.' Brinley Richards and Lindsay Sloper were among his English pupils. Otto Goldschmidt, the husband of Jenny Lind, knew Tellefsen, a Norwegian, and declared that he had given 'the only correct and true edition of Chopin's works.' However this may be, none of Chopin's pupils ever communicated the Chopin secret. Perhaps, indeed, as Sir Henry Hadow says, the Chopin secret was incommunicable—something too intimate and personal to be expressed in the concrete language of principle and formula.

And that brings us to the consideration more particularly of Chopin himself as a player. He played as he composed—uniquely. James Huneker sums him up in this character in a few sentences:

Scales that were pearls, a touch rich, sweet, supple and ringing, and a technique that knew no difficulties — these were part of Chopin's equipment as a pianist. He spiritualized the timbre of his instrument until it became transformed into something strange, something remote from its original nature. His *pianissimo* was an enchanting whisper; his *forte* seemed powerful by contrast, so numberless were the gradations, so widely varied his dynamics. The fairylike quality of his play, his diaphanous harmonies, his liquid tone, his pedalling—all were the work of a genius and a

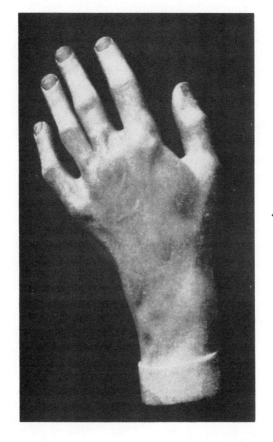

CHOPIN'S HAND

From a Marble in the National Museum at Budapest

lifetime; and the appealing humanity he infused into his touch gave his listeners a delight that bordered on the supernatural.

So the accounts, critical, professional and personal, read. Mendelssohn called him 'radically original.' Lenz described him as 'a phoenix of intimacy with the piano.' Meyerbeer declared that he knew nobody like him. Lord Houghton, who heard him in Paris, spoke of the strange pathos with which his hands 'meandered over the piano.' 'The evenness of his scales and passages in all kinds of touch was,' says Mikuli, 'unsurpassed, nay prodigious.' And so on without end.[1]

The chief feature of his style, his delicacy of tone, has been remarked upon in the course of the biography. In a very small measure it may have been traceable to his frail physique. Heller told Niecks that in his last days his playing was sometimes barely audible, and that merely because of his weakness. We must, however, remember that it was quality of tone not quantity that he sought. 'My manner of playing pleases the ladies so much,' he said in 1829. This manner he retained to the end. Heine called him the poet of the piano; somebody else has called him the Tennyson of the instrument. His style was excellent for the drawing-room, but it prevented his making an effect with the public. His indifferent health may have had something to do with the dislike he entertained of the crowd. 'It is a dreadful time for me,' he said, speaking of the week or more before a concert; 'I do not like public life, but it is part of my profession.' Liszt suggests that the feeling was due to the fact that the conviction of his own superiority 'did not meet with the sufficient reverberation and

[1] There is an excellent description of his playing in Marion Crawford's romance, *The Immortals*.

echo from without to give him what he required—namely, the calm assurance that he was perfectly appreciated.' But this is not a satisfactory explanation. The truth is, of course, that the Chopin temperament was incompatible with the excite-ments of the public concert room. It shone on the keyboard only in private, among friends and admirers. 'To be heard to advantage,' said his friend Osborne, 'he required a small and select company of connoisseurs, who could appreciate in his cabinet pictures, as Liszt calls his shorter pieces, all the poetic refinement which was his peculiar characteristic.' All the best accounts which we have of his playing come from those who heard him *en petit cercle des amateurs.* Mathias says: 'Those who heard Chopin play may well say they never heard anything approaching his playing. It was like his music: and what virtuosity! what strength! what force! But it lasted only several minutes. In the presence of women Chopin surpassed himself, especially when they had titles.'

All this more particularly as regards the delicacy of his tone. But Chopin did not always play quite in the same manner. He played as the mood prompted him. Mikuli asserts that he brought out an 'immense tone' in *cantabile.* In the *salon* he could be elegant, brilliant, coquettish. But he had 'dark moments, when the keyboard was too small, his ideas too big for utterance. Then he astounded, thrilled his auditors.' Liszt says that when he was strong he used a Pleyel piano, when he was ill an Erard. He liked the Erard, but preferred the Pleyel for its 'veiled sonority.' If he was engaged to play at a house where there was no Pleyel he would sometimes send his own instrument. When Mendelssohn heard him first, he wrote: 'There is something so thoroughly original and masterly about his pianoforte playing, that he may be called a truly perfect virtuoso.'

Moscheles tried some of his works in 1833 and declared
that his fingers stuck and stumbled at certain passages which,
practise as he might, he could never play fluently. When six
years later he heard Chopin himself play, he wrote rather
differently. 'The *ad libitum,*' he said, 'which with Chopin's
interpreters degenerate into bad time, is, in his own hands,
the most charming originality of execution; the harsh and
dilettante-like modulations which I could never get over when
playing his compositions ceased to offend when his delicate
fairy fingers glided over them. He is quite unique in the
pianistic world.' This from Moscheles, a rival, is noteworthy.
His reference to Chopin's 'fairy fingers' reminds one of
Stephen Heller's remark. 'It was,' he said, 'a wonderful
sight to see Chopin's small hand expand and cover a third of
the keyboard. It was like the opening of the mouth of a
serpent about to swallow a rabbit whole.' It is said that he
could stretch tenths with ease: his first Study indeed indicates
as much.

From his earliest years he had delighted in extended *arpeggio*
chords, and to render them easier of execution he invented a
mechanical contrivance, which he kept between his fingers
during the night—a contrivance which seems to have been
rewarded with more success than Schumann's attempt to
increase the independence of the fingers by similar means.
Those who have played his eleventh Study, in E flat major,
will appreciate the advantage of having supple fingers with
increased space between them. Osborne, who resided quite
near him in Paris and had the advantage of hearing him play
many of his compositions while still in manuscript, says that
'the great steadiness of his accompaniment, whether with the
right or left hand, was truly remarkable.' Even into his
printed works he would introduce *fioriture,* always varying

them when repeated with new embroideries, according to the fancy of the moment. In bravura passages he would sing out loudly, exclaiming: 'This will require force and dash,' evidently having Liszt in his mind.

Otto Goldschmidt, who heard him at his last concert in Paris, declared that he possessed in an almost unique degree the faculty of passing upwards from *piano* through all gradations of tone. He mentions another point which demands some consideration. Chopin's employment of what is known as *tempo rubato* has been much written about. Goldschmidt, agreeing therein with Osborne, says that his *rubato* playing was really no *rubato* playing at all: his left hand kept a very distinct rhythm and perfect time, whilst the right hand performed independently, just as a finished vocalist would sing properly supported by a sympathetic accompanist. Critics who did not understand his style spoke of Chopin's 'exaggerated phrasing.' Hanslick referred to it as a 'morbid unsteadiness of tempo.' But it is perfectly clear that, while he looked to the *tempo rubato* as a means of emotional expression, Chopin never intended that it should obscure the rhythm. One hand might be unfettered; it must be the function of the other to mark the beat. 'Time is the soul of music,' he said. 'Let your left hand be your conductor and always keep time,' was one of Mozart's injunctions. It must have been one of Chopin's injunctions too. Friederike Streicher, one of his pupils, tells us that 'he required adherence to the strictest rhythm, hated all lingering and lagging and misplaced *rubati,* as well as exaggerated *ritardandi.*' We have read Chorley's statement that he could be 'as staid as a metronome' in compositions not his own. Berlioz's assertion that he could not keep time is ridiculous. The *tempo rubato* is an essential of the Chopin style, an essential which he tried to impart to his pupils; but Liszt is doubtless right in saying that it is difficult for those who never heard him play to catch its true secret.

In the matter of the employment of the pedal Chopin was equally original. Rubinstein declared all the pedal marks in the published editions of his works to be wrong. The statement is a characteristic exaggeration, but it finds some support in the evidence of those who could speak with authority of Chopin's own employment of the pedal. It was Chopin, says W. J. Henderson,[1] who 'systematized the art of pedalling and showed us how to use both pedals in combination to produce those wonderful effects of colour, which are so necessary in the performance of his music.' How much more did Chopin show this by his own practice at the keyboard. No system of marking could ever bring out his effects in all their details. The older virtuosi used the pedals merely for contrasts of *piano* and *forte*: Chopin used them as a painter uses his colours, enriching by their means those peculiar extended harmonies of his compositions, so that they vibrate all through with the fundamental tone. Another point is noted by Charles Willeby. For the purpose of gaining an exceptional *legato* effect Chopin often used the pedal immediately after striking the chord, in the manner indicated in the following illustration (page 166), where the pressing down of the pedal is shown by the quaver and its release by the quaver rest.

The pedal, so important an agent in elucidating the composer's meaning and in rendering the tone plastic, becomes, through improper use, like a wet sponge rudely passed over a beautiful picture. It has been said that language was given to man to conceal his thoughts. With a great number of

[1] *How Music Developed*, by W. J. Henderson (London, 1899). The whole of chapter viii, on 'The Evolution of Piano Playing,' might be read in this connection.

pianists the pedals serve exactly that purpose. With Chopin, the greatest master in their refined use, they were second only to the keyboard itself.

So far nothing has been said of Chopin as an extemporizer. Extemporizing has gone out of fashion now, unless perhaps at organ recitals, but in Chopin's day an improvisation was generally a feature of every virtuoso's programme. Chopin began to improvise very early, and he improvised all his life. Those who heard him say that his improvisations were just like his written compositions; indeed in a sense many of his compositions are but improvisations with the pen. George

Sand says that his creativeness 'descended upon his piano suddenly, completely, sublimely, or it sang itself in his head during his walks, and he made haste to hear it by rushing to the instrument.' One can hardly fancy Chopin composing away from the keyboard, turning over his melodic ideas in his head, according to the Schumann precept, until he could say to himself: 'It is well done.' A Beethoven or a Bach might do that; hardly a Chopin. No doubt melodies came to Chopin away from the piano, but he probably picked them out at the instrument more easily than without its aid. His improvisations at any rate suggested as much. He could improvise, says Osborne, 'to an unlimited extent, producing the most marvellous effects.'

Another feature of his playing may be noted. Chopin, writes Count Tarnowski,

liked and knew how to express individual characteristics on the piano. Just as there formerly was a rather widely-known fashion of describing dispositions and characters in so-called 'portraits,' which gave to ready wits a scope for parading their knowledge of people and their sharpness of observation, so he often amused himself by playing such musical portraits. Without saying whom he had in his thoughts he illustrated the characters of a few or of several people present in the room, illustrating them so clearly and so delicately that the listeners could always guess correctly who was intended.

Tarnowski proceeds to recite an absurd tale of how Chopin once represented the Countess Delphine Potocka on the piano. He

drew her shawl from her shoulders, threw it on the keyboard and began to play, implying in this two things: first, that he knew the character of the brilliant and famous queen of fashion so well that by heart and in the dark he was able to depict it; secondly, that this character and this soul is hidden under habits, ornamentations and decorations of an elegant worldly life, through the symbol of elegance and fashion of that day, as the tones of the piano through the shawl.

This is a very good specimen of the romantic rubbish that has been written about Chopin. Here it is quite enough to record that he had the talent for mimicry. Balzac alludes to it in his novel *Un Homme d'affaires,* where he remarks of one of the characters that 'he is endowed with the same gift of imitating people which Chopin, the pianist, possesses in so high a degree.' Liszt, who was himself a victim—when his back was turned—says that he often amused himself by 'reproducing the musical formulas and peculiar tricks of virtuosi in burlesque and most comical improvisations, imitating their gestures and movements and counterfeiting their faces with a cleverness which at once depicted their entire personality.' Liszt adds that at such times his own features were scarcely recognizable, as he could impose on them the 'strongest metamorphoses.' Nowakowski, again, relates how he once asked Chopin to make him acquainted with Liszt, Kalkbrenner and others. 'That is not necessary,' said Chopin, who, seating himself at the piano, imitated each of the men named in manner, gesture and style of playing and composition.

If one could only hear Chopin's works now as he played them himself! I have commented on the fact that none of his pupils gave the Chopin tradition to the musical world. Indeed, nobody seems agreed as to what the Chopin tradition is, or rather was. James Huneker says that the Slavic and Magyar races are the only true Chopin interpreters. Witness Liszt, Rubinstein, Tausig, Paderewski, Pachmann, Joseffy and Rosenthal. And yet probably not one of these revealed, or reveals, the real Chopin. Even Huneker admits that when Rubinstein, Tausig and Liszt played Chopin in 'passional phrases' the public and critics were aghast. Theirs was too often a transformed Chopin—a Chopin transposed to a key of manliness which was not in his nature. Chopin's pupils declined to accept Rubinstein as an interpreter. His touch was 'too rich and full, his tone too big.' Charles Hallé heard Chopin at his last concert in Paris; when, later on, he heard Rubinstein do 'all sorts of wonderful things' with the coda of the *Barcarolle,* he said it was 'clever but not Chopinesque.' In short, only Chopin knew how to play Chopin.

CHAPTER XII

THERE is no style of music that is better known to the musician and the amateur than that of Chopin. Yet when one sits down to write of it, to try to analyse it, to say exactly what are its essential characteristics, to what it owes its peculiar fascination, it is then that one feels the inadequacy of language. True, the grammarian might go through it, classify all its progressions and label all its chords. There is no more reason why this analytical process should not be possible with Chopin's music than with Bach's or Mendelssohn's. But the result of such a process would be mainly a negative one. It would show that Chopin was not a great master of form in the larger sense, not a skilled contrapuntist, not a deep thinker with a message. It would show, indeed, that he was a master of melody and an innovator in harmony, but it would help us not a whit to understand the qualities which make him unique. His spirit is 'too volatile for our clumsy alembics, too intangible for our concrete methods of investigation. It eludes our glance, it vanishes at our touch, it mocks with a foregone failure all our efforts at description or analysis.'

To some who know it only superficially it may seem easy enough to characterize the music of Chopin in general terms. Its extraordinary beauty and finish are perhaps the leading qualities. One thinks instinctively of Tennyson—the Tennyson of *The Princess,* in which we have the best words best placed and that curious felicity of style which strikes instantly.

and without cavil as the perfection of art. 'Load every rift with ore' was the advice which Keats gave to Shelley. In Chopin it is as if every rift had been consciously loaded with ore. Not a single bar seems to be wanting, not a single bar seems to be redundant. There is no commonplace, nothing stale, nothing hackneyed, nothing vulgar. The perfection of form, the complexity of figure, the delicate elaboration of ornament, the rich harmonic colouring, the fine polish of phrase, the winning melody, the keen vital quality of passion, the grace and the tenderness—these at least can be pointed out in terms of everyday vocabulary.

I have mentioned Keats and Shelley. In the music of Chopin there is something of the spirit of both. Chopin's world, like Shelley's, is a region 'where music and moonlight and feeling are one'—a fairy realm where nothing seems familiar. Both look upon a night of 'cloudless climes and starry skies.' The warmth, the spirituality, the colour of the romance spirit is in the one as in the other. We note the ethereal grace of both, the beautiful images, the exquisite, if sometimes far-drawn, fancies. Like Keats, Chopin often sees

> . . . magic casements, opening on the foam
> Of perilous seas, in faëry lands forlorn.

His philosophy is of the beautiful, as is Keats's; he is nature's 'most exquisite sounding-board, and vibrates to her with intensity, colour and vivacity that have no parallel.' A whole volume might be written about Chopin the composer. The essence of the matter is here. Chopin is pure emotion. 'Make me thy lyre,' he might have prayed to the spirit of Poesy. His music is all expressive of moods, of phases of feeling, now strenuous, now morbid, now tender, now simply tricksy. There is nothing of Bach's calm dignity or Beethoven's

171

titanic energy; you find no traces of intellectual wrestling, of thoughts too deep for tears; you find instead tears that are, perhaps, a little too facile, like the tears of women, the cause not always commensurate with their copiousness. There is gaiety, yearning, pathos, but nothing that even touches sublimity, little that stirs one to the healthful activity that is the true life of man. Chopin's music is, first and last, emotion surcharged, not intellectualized, not finding its legitimate development into action. As with Chopin the player, so with Chopin the composer: he stands alone. He is the one master *sui generis,* a genius for whom the music critic and historian has no pigeon-hole in his bureau of classified composers. His art ended with him. As he sprang from no existing school, so he founded no school. It is this absolutely unique quality of his music which has preserved him so effectually against the flattery of imitation. His work is entirely beyond the reach of the imitator. Its charm is so wholly personal to himself that only another Chopin, like him in all things—in temperament, in bias, in environment, in emotion, in experience—could hope to reproduce it. Followers he no doubt has had. But the follower can at best copy only the method, and Chopin had practically no method. What he had was a manner.

It has been remarked that as a pianist Chopin was less successful on the concert platform than when playing to a select circle of friends. The conditions may be said to apply to his music, though not to the same extent. That Chopin's music makes a large part of the stock-in-trade of the concert pianist is, of course, true. Yet it can hardly be denied that even in the hands of the same interpreter the emotional effect of many of the compositions is greater when these compositions are heard in a private room than in a concert hall. Much of the subtle and sensuous harmony seems to be lost in large surroundings and in the presence of a large audience.

And here I am reminded of the fact that Chopin's strongest appeal can only be to certain natures, to one type of mind and to one mood of that mind. 'He is,' writes Francis Hueffer, 'the representative of a decaying nation, and his individual genius is tinged with melancholy to a degree which to a robust and healthy nature might well appear in the light of a disease.' He has been bracketed by some writers with the 'sick men'—whoever they may be—and his entire musical product has been called morbid, sickly, unwholesome. 'It may be feverish,' says a prominent English critic, 'merely mournful, . . . or tranquil, and entirely beautiful. . . . It is marvellous music, but all the same it is sick, unhealthy music.' Heinrich Pudor, who describes Wagner as 'a thorough-going decadent,' declares that the figure of Chopin the composer comes before one 'as flesh without bones—this morbid, womanly, womanish, slip-slop, powerless, bleached, sweet-caramel Pole.'

This is the sort of person who would look for genius only in the full red cheeks and the expansive waistcoat. But even for invalidism one might find something to say. Some of the finest things in art and literature have been done by people who were in more or less delicate health. Pope spoke of 'that long disease, my life.' Mere valetudinarianism seems to have been the inspirer of much that is admirable in prose and verse. Invalidism has been the motive, or at any rate the marked accompaniment, of a great deal that is effective and even charming in art and literature. It is from the minds of women poets not physically robust that have come most of those 'airs and floating echoes' which 'convey a melancholy unto all our day.' *Wuthering Heights,* one of the strongest

173

pieces of fiction ever done by a woman's pen, was conceived and written under the shadow of death. That Chopin was a consumptive is nothing. Perhaps, if he had not been a consumptive, oblivion would long ago have covered him. But that is another of the ineffectual 'ifs.'

Personally, I think that far too much is made of Chopin's melancholy. Chopin, said one of his own friends, 'had a cheerful mind but a sad heart.' Chopin's music is a compound of the same contradictions—of cheerfulness and sadness. Without doubt, nature had tuned him in a minor key; but just as in everyday life he had his gay moments, so in his music we find moments of light-heartedness, moments of humour I had almost said, when life seems worth living, and this world something better than a charnel-house. If we knew all the circumstances connected with the inception of his various works we should probably find that what is sorrowful in them was written during his gloomy, sentimental moods. When he composed in a bright mood he could be as bright as anybody else.

His early works in particular show sprightliness and vivacity —the Variations on the *Don Giovanni* theme,[1] for instance. Look at the Rondos, Op. 5 and Op. 16, at the Fantasy on Polish Airs, at the two concertos. There is no sadness or despair in these; rather youth, exuberance of life, happiness and elation, love of mankind. In the Fantasy, Op. 13, there is a note of melancholy, but the impression is not lasting: a long shake, a few chords, and we are in a brisk country dance. There is fire and cheerfulness in the grand Polonaise in A flat major, written in Paris; the Concert Allegro, Op. 46, is full of life and verve. The mazurkas, the national dances of Poland, a little more than half of which are in minor keys,

[1] *Là ci darem la mano.*

are by no means all sad. On the contrary, some have quite a warlike ardour. The minor key of the Polish dances is neither unhappy nor macabre. 'A fig for wretchedness!' says a national proverb. The Polish peasants are happiest when they sing in the minor mode.

The nocturnes, again, have a character at variance with the idea that the composer, from first to last, was the enervated, broken creature so often depicted. No doubt they are heavily charged with sentiment, but it is not a sickly sentiment. Similarly with the preludes. Many people imagine that they see in these evidences of his misery at Majorca. But, suppose he was unhappy in what may be called his domestic relations: so was Haydn, and yet he is not found, if the expression may be allowed, washing dirty linen in his works. There is too much reading into Chopin's compositions of the personal states and physical condition of the man. 'Poor fellow! he was a consumptive!' That is the key which unlocks the alleged melancholy. There is melancholy in Chopin, certainly. But what I mean is that a great many people find him all melancholy who would have found no melancholy in him at all if he had been a portly, roast-beef Englishman— if such a supposition be admissible.

But, when all is said and done, we come back to our original assertion that Chopin's strongest appeal can only be to those of strongly sensuous, emotional, impressionable temperament. 'I do not care for the ladies' Chopin,' said Wagner; 'there is too much of the Parisian *salon* in that.' The statement involves no reflection on Wagner, any more than it involved a reflection on Chopin that he did not care for the occasionally boisterous gaiety of Schubert. Even as long ago as 1841 the conditions necessary for a full appreciation of Chopin were understood. In that year a Parisian critic wrote: 'In order to appreciate him rightly one must love gentle impressions and have the feeling for poetry.' That puts the matter in a nutshell. And just as Chopin can only appeal to certain natures, so he can only be interpreted through the keyboard by players who, in addition to the peculiar temperament demanded, have the special kind of technique and touch which is necessary. Something has been said of this in dealing with Chopin himself as a player. It was remarked by a Frenchman of his own time that to hear Chopin rightly interpreted was to read a strophe of Lamartine. But how seldom do we hear him rightly interpreted! The 'conscientious and heavy-handed pianist' attacks him and crushes him out of all recognition. 'Solidity of execution' may serve for several composers in the virtuoso's repertory, but solidity of execution must prove absolutely fatal in the case of Chopin. The daintiest delicacy of touch is required for these airy creatures of his, for that filigree work which decks his scores. They are conceived in the poetic, let us even say in the minstrel spirit, and are no more to be rendered with scientific exactness than are the gipsy songs of the Hungarians. You cannot make the ideal Chopin interpreter. Like the poet, he must be born.

To trace the influences which helped to form Chopin's style as a composer for the keyboard is almost futile. His style was his own from the beginning. As one may see the Tennyson of *In Memoriam* and the *Idylls* in the early poems of his Cambridge days, so in the first of the Chopin compositions we recognize the peculiarities of the Chopin manner. Practically there was no development. We talk of Beethoven's three styles, and the merest amateur knows that the Wagner of *Rienzi* is not the Wagner of *Tristan*. In the Verdi of *Il Trovatore* and *La Traviata* who would have thought to find the Verdi of *Otello* and *Falstaff*?

Chopin presents no such study of evolution. Of all the great masters—the adjective may be allowed for the present—he is the one who showed the most originality from the start. Handel, Beethoven, Haydn, Schumann, Schubert, Mendelssohn—in the tentative works of all these one can clearly discern the influence of their predecessors. Wagner wrote his early and only Symphony with more than one model before him, and his first operatic works betrayed allegiance to Meyerbeer, [Weber, Marschner, Spontini and others.] From the first Chopin struck out on his own path. As by a natural intuition he 'seized at once on the most adequate mode of expressing his thoughts, and never changed it.' No doubt, if it were worth while attempting the task, one might make him out a debtor in certain small details. Schumann said of him: 'He studied from the very best models': he took from Beethoven 'temerity and inspiration, from Schubert tenderness of feeling, from Field manual dexterity.' But this can be accepted only in the most general way, as one would accept the statement that Beethoven was indebted to Bach, or Pope to Spenser and Dryden. 'We are all literary cannibals and feed on each other,' says Oliver Wendell Holmes. Chopin fed upon those who had gone before him, but the assimilation was so perfect that, to carry the metaphor a little further, his music shows no more of its original constituents than did Holmes's physical body of the sheep and oxen on which it was sustained. His obligation to Hummel and to John Field have often been insisted upon,[1] but I think this can only apply to the very earliest of his compositions. From

[1] The influence of Bellini on Chopin's melody is not to be overlooked. A slow air from a Bellini opera, played rather freely and with a more pianistic accompaniment, sounds remarkably like a Chopin nocturne.—E. B.

Field he got his idea of the nocturnes, but the limpid style of that neglected composer would have come out in Chopin though Field had never written a bar of music.

It is more to the point to trace the influences on his style of his beloved Poland's folksong. In his young days he was much in the country listening to the fiddling and the singing of the peasants. In this way he indirectly laid the corner-stone of his art as a national composer. I say a national composer advisedly, for so Chopin regarded himself. It was an aspiration with him from the first to put Poland, as it were, into his music. 'I should like,' he said, 'to be to my people what Uhland is to the Germans.' To be sure, the external qualities of his music are all his own. But the texture is essentially of native growth and native substance.

Sir Henry Hadow brings this out more clearly and with more detail than any other writer who has touched upon the subject. He shows that there are three separate ways in which the national influence affected Chopin's work. In the first place, it determined the main forms of his art-product. The popular music of Poland is almost invariably founded on dance forms and dance rhythms: more than a quarter of Chopin's entire composition is devoted ostensibly to dance forms, and throughout the rest of it their effect may be seen in a hundred phrases and episodes. A second point of resemblance is Chopin's habit of 'founding a whole paragraph either on a single phrase repeated in similar shapes, or on two phrases in alternation.' This is a very primitive practice, for which no artistic value can be claimed on its own merits. But 'when it is confined to an episodic passage, especially in a composition founded on a striking or important melody, it may serve as a very justifiable point of rest, a background of which the interest is purposely toned down to provide a more striking contrast with the central figure.'

It is in the mazurkas that we find this practice most successfully employed—particularly in the first (in F sharp minor), the fifth (in B flat major) and the thirty-seventh (in A flat major). Thirdly, Chopin was to a considerable extent affected by the tonality of his native music. The larger number of the Polish folksongs are written, not in our modern scale, but in one or other of the medieval Church modes—the Dorian, the Lydian and the rest. Moreover, some of them end on what we should call dominant harmony. Of this modal system, as Hadow shows, some positive traces may be found in the mazurkas, the cadences of the thirteenth, seventeenth and twenty-fifth, the frequent use of a sharpened subdominant, and the like; while on the negative side it may perhaps account for Chopin's indifference to the requirements of key relationship. The latter is an unusually interesting point. In several of his works widely separated keys are brought into the closest relationship; many of his modulations are as inexplicable on theoretical grounds as those of the average church organist who, in his flights of improvisation, smothers the tone in the swell-box and allows the new key to emerge from the obscurity. Something of all this might perhaps be set to the account of the romantic movement. But I think Sir Henry Hadow is right in seeing a special reason beyond, in the fact that Chopin approached our Western key system from the outside and never wholly assimilated himself to the method of thought which it implies.

This seems to be the place for some remarks on what may be termed the theoretical aspect of Chopin's works. The perfect fit of his form to his individual requirements has already been hinted at, and indeed there is little to add on the point.

Chopin

Chopin was as finical about the form of his compositions as he was about his dress and personal appearance; and when one has said that with him there is no padding, no commonplace, that 'every effect is studied with deliberate purpose and wrought to the highest degree of finish that it can bear,' one finds it unnecessary to step over to the grey borderland of pedagogy.

His harmonies must have been the horror of the old schoolmen. Genius makes its own laws, but never before did genius defy the formulas of the theory books as Chopin did. He was in many ways distinctly in advance of his time. The great chords in the B minor Scherzo (Op. 20) are Wagnerian before Wagner. In one of the Studies (the D flat major, Op. 25, No. 8) there is a remarkable passage of consecutive fifths which must have staggered the pundits more than anything that Beethoven or Wagner ever dared. Consecutive major thirds appear in another Study—the one in A flat major without Opus number. In certain of the other compositions there are combinations which, far as we have travelled on the theoretical road since Chopin's day, still excite marvel. Established distinctions between concord and discord are ignored with an audacity that had then no parallel in the history of the art. It has been hinted in explanation of these and other vagaries that Chopin's theoretical training was imperfect. There is no ground for a suggestion of the kind, but if there were we should reject it simply because the end in Chopin justifies the means. There is not a solitary instance in which his infractions of accepted rules fail of their effect. They ought to be ugly; in his hands they are beautiful. Doubtless in another style of music they would be less welcome to the ear. The Chopin harmonic idiom goes with the Chopin manner. It is not to be regarded in the orthodox fashion.

Rather may we liken it to a river—'its surface wind-swept into a thousand variable crests and eddies, its current moving onward, full, steadfast and inevitable, bearing the whole volume of its waters by sheer force of depth and impetus.'

It is a subject of remark with all writers on Chopin that he never once attempted choral composition and such of the larger forms of his art as the symphony, the overture and the opera. By some critics this is regarded as a reproach. It is really no reproach. Chopin knew his own craft and kept to it. Shelley once said that it was as vain to ask for human interest in his poems as to seek to buy a leg of mutton in a gin-shop. It is all but certain that as a composer of opera Chopin would have been a total failure; it is entirely certain that if he had attempted the symphony he would have altogether overstepped the bounds of his genius. His genius was essentially lyric-elegiac, not epic, nor even truly dramatic. As his character was deficient in virility, so his muse must have broken down under a big undertaking. Technique aside, he lacked that power of concentrated effort, that sustaining quality, which must be the possession of the composer who would successfully work out primary ideas to their logical and inevitable conclusion on a large scale. His thoughts were excellent, his original ideas in the way of themes were excellent, but they depended greatly upon the clothing given them on the keyboard and on the peculiar genius of the instrument. They could never have been heard to advantage in orchestral guise. The delicate embroideries, the pedal effects, the broken arpeggios and scale passages, are all quite unsuited to orchestral work and totally unfitted for orchestral treatment. Chopin always thought in terms of the piano: he had no orchestral sense and comparatively little orchestral technique. In his two concertos the piano is everything; the orchestration is such as might have been written by a Bachelor of Music. It is crude and absolutely unorchestral. Deficiency of technique, it must be insisted, does not account entirely for this: the main reason is that Chopin's ideas themselves were not orchestral. His orchestration has been retouched by adepts of the art, but it remains unsatisfactory.

The point need not be laboured. In these things there are compensations. Had Chopin been a great master of the orchestra, it is more than probable that his piano music would not have been the unique product it is. If one may dare say it, even Beethoven was often too orchestral in his piano music. Brahms's heavy chords in the lower register of the piano may have been intended as an attempt at certain orchestral effects, but the attempt cannot be called successful. Liszt, too, had severe limitations: the larger works which he essayed proved that he lacked the technical training necessary to develop in a natural way. Like Chopin in his concertos, he was out of his depth. To Chopin is really due, as Hans von Bülow has said, the honour and credit of having set fast the boundary between piano and orchestral music, which through other composers of the romantic school, Schumann especially, was in danger of being blotted out, to the prejudice and damage of both species.

If Chopin was small in great things he was great in small things. He was a composer for the piano and for the piano alone. His style is suited to it and to no other instrument whatever. He cannot be arranged, as most of the great masters, from Handel to Wagner, have been arranged. Divorce him from the keyboard and you rob him of his native tongue. It is as if Paganini had been set to play the oboe or the horn. Rubinstein said finely: 'The piano bard, the piano rhapsodist, the piano mind, the piano soul is Chopin. Tragic, romantic, lyric, heroic, dramatic, fantastic, soulful, sweet, dreamy, brilliant, grand, simple: all possible expressions are found in his compositions, and all are sung by him upon his instrument.' In a lesser man this oneness would have led to monotony: in him it led to concentration of the very highest order. He scaled no Alpine heights of art. He worked in a small field—a personality graceful without strength, romantic without the sense of tragedy, highly dowered with all gentle qualities of nature, but lacking in the more virile powers, in breadth of vision, in epic magnanimity, in massive force. We may not call him a great composer: we cannot deny his claim to genius. The great composers went their way; Chopin went his. He lived his life, gave what was in him, and died with a name destined, like the name of Mary Stuart, to exert over unborn generations a witchery and a charm unique in the history of his art.

CHAPTER XIII

THE COMPOSITIONS

CHOPIN, more than any other, composed in groups. The nocturnes, the polonaises, the mazurka, the studies, the preludes—these go together in clusters. They constitute the main body of his work, and show the most characteristic features of his art. One would like to deal with each of these categories in technical detail, but that is obviously impossible in the space at command. Those who desire to have something more than the general summary which can be attempted here should read the published lectures of Jan Kleczynski,[1] and the analytical part of James Huneker's biography of the composer. The latter, to which I have been much indebted, is admirable and especially valuable to the student for the attention the author gives to questions of fingering and phrasing.

The first work of which we have any definite information was the March composed for the Grand Duke Constantine when Chopin was just ten. The duke was evidently pleased with this juvenile production, since he had it scored for, and played by, one of the military bands. Of course, it was not dignified by an Opus number. The actual Op. 1, the Rondo

[1] (1) *The Works of Chopin and their Proper Interpretation*, by J. Kleczynski. Translated by A. Whittingham (London, n.d.). (2) *Chopin's Greater Works : How they should be Understood*, by J. Kleczynski. Translated by Natalie Janotha (London, 1896).

for piano in C minor, dedicated to Madame de Linde, is assigned to the year 1825. But in the list of posthumous publications without opus number there is a Polonaise in G sharp minor, conjecturally assigned to 1822. That is the date of the Breitkopf & Härtel edition of the work; and, moreover, the Warsaw edition has the following note: 'So far as one can judge from the manuscript and its dedication, this composition was written by Frederic Chopin at the age of fourteen, and never published until now.' This is, however, as Charles Willeby remarks, by no means convincing; and a careful examination of the work itself certainly inclines one to believe that it must have been composed considerably later. The Rondo in C minor is very creditable for an Opus 1. It is melodious, as a matter of course, and admirably adapted to the instrument of the composer's choice. The form is perhaps redundant and ill-balanced, but, as Tennyson said in another connection, allowance must be made for the abundance of youth. The other rondos are more inviting, particularly the one in F major for piano and orchestra (Op. 14), known as the *Krakowiak*. That in F major (Op. 5) is interesting as showing the development of the composer's style. The one in C major for two pianos (Op. 73), a posthumous publication, is in the nature of a show-piece.

Opus 2 was published in 1830. This was the famous Variations in B flat major for piano with orchestral accompaniment on Mozart's *Là ci darem la mano*, which called forth the oft-quoted eulogy of Schumann: 'Hats off, gentlemen: a genius!' It was the first journalistic recognition of Chopin as a composer, and it speaks eloquently for Schumann's discrimination and generosity. Chopin wrote other variations, but he was not very successful in this department. 'The composer runs down the theme with roulades, and throttles and hangs it with chains of shakes,' said Rellstab, and he was not far wrong. The best thing that can be said for Chopin's variations, indeed, is that they were immensely superior to those of Herz, which at that time enjoyed a tremendous vogue.

The two concertos, the one in E minor and the other in F minor, were among the earlier works. They need not detain us. The weakness of the orchestration, which seldom rises beyond mere accompaniment, and the want of variety of key have already been noted. Chopin lacked the power of organic development of themes and strict working out of motifs. As Ehlert says:

Noblesse oblige, and thus Chopin felt himself compelled to satisfy all demands exacted of a pianist, and wrote the unavoidable Concerto. It was not consistent with his nature to express himself in broad terms. His lungs were too weak for the pace in seven-league boots, so often required in a score. The Trio and cello Sonata were also tasks for whose accomplishment nature did not design him.

Of the three sonatas the same thing might be said. The first, in C minor (Op. 4), was written as early as 1827, though not published till 1851. It is a dull work, showing but little of the essential characteristics of the composer. The second, the B flat minor Sonata (Op. 35), appeared in 1840. Schumann said of this work that Chopin had here 'bound together four of his maddest children': a pregnant remark. The four movements, regarded separately, are admirable, but taken together they have little thematic or other affinity. The *Marche funèbre,* which constitutes the third movement, has been popularized to death, though Schumann found in it 'much that is repulsive.' It is really the finest movement in the Sonata. The third Sonata, in B minor (Op. 58), though attractive to pianists for the bravura nature of the finale, is an inferior work,[1] notwithstanding that it has more organic unity than the others. With these three sonatas we may include the Sonata in G minor (Op. 65) for piano and cello. There is some beautiful music in this work, and it is congenial to the cello, but on the whole it is only another evidence of Chopin's inability to deal successfully with the sonata form. That unity of feeling which ought to pervade an entire sonata was apparently not at his command.

Among the fantasies the one which first claims attention is that in A major on Polish Airs (Op. 13). This was a favourite of the composer himself, who often played it. It is one of his most brilliant works, showing him in quite another character from that of the sad and melancholy Pole of whom the world has heard so much. The orchestration is perhaps more successful here, so far as it goes, than in any of his other works. The F minor Fantasy (Op. 49) is, in many respects, the grandest of all his compositions—'one of the greatest of piano pieces,' says James Huneker. To Niecks it suggests a Titan in commotion. It is his largest canvas, and 'more nearly approaches Beethoven in its unity, its formal rectitude and its brave economy of thematic material.' Chopin had a 'programme' for it, but it must mean different things to different people.

Of the four scherzos one might write at some length. They are not scherzos in the Beethovenian sense of the term. The Beethoven scherzo is 'full of a robust sort of humour.' In these scherzos of Chopin we have the composer in all his

---

[1] It is not an editor's duty to interfere with an author's opinions, as distinct from his statements of fact. Nevertheless, it is difficult to let so harsh a judgment of the B minor Sonata stand without a mild protest.—E. B.

moods, from grave to gay, from merry to melancholy. Rubinstein greatly admired the first and the second—the B minor
(Op. 20) and the B flat minor (Op. 31). In the B minor
one cannot help noticing the extraordinary opening—the two
discords, very unusual and bold at that time. To Schumann
the B flat minor Scherzo recommended itself for its Byronic
tenderness and boldness. Lenz quotes Chopin as saying of
the opening: 'It must be a charnel-house.' But Ehlert says
it was 'composed in a blessed hour.' The third Scherzo, in
C sharp minor (Op. 39), is the most dramatic of the four, and
perhaps bears out its title better than any of the others. It was
dedicated to Gutmann, because, as Lenz relates, Gutmann
had a fist which could 'knock a hole in the table' with a
certain chord in the sixth bar. This was one of the Majorca
works—either written or finished there. The Scherzo in E
major (Op. 54) is notable for delicacy of treatment, but the
effect is rather marred by its excessive length.

The *Berceuse* (Op. 57) and the *Barcarolle* (Op. 60) may be
bracketed together. The first was called by Dumas *fils*
'muted music.' It is, indeed, a lovely composition, a true
cradle song, delicate and dreamy, in the master's very best
manner. The *Barcarolle*—singular in being in 12-8 time—
has been described as 'a nocturne painted on a large canvas
with larger brushes.' Tausig, who played it superbly, found
in it a tender dialogue between a lover and his lass in a discreet
gondola. It is certainly a two-voiced composition, but we
cannot be sure that Chopin had any idea of a love duet in
his mind.

In addition to these we have the *Bolero* (Op. 19) and the
Tarantella in A flat major (Op. 43). The one ought to have
a Spanish, the other an Italian flavour, but Chopin could not
get away from Poland. The form is here, but the spirit is

wanting. It was of the *Tarantella* that Schumann declared: 'Nobody can call that music.' The seventeen Polish Songs (Op. 74) were written between 1824 and 1844 to words by Mickiewicz, Krasinski, Witwicki and others. With one or two exceptions, they do not represent the composer at a high level. The best known is *The Maiden's Wish,* which was brilliantly paraphrased by Liszt.

Now let us consider the groups. First of all we may take the waltzes. Though Schubert and Weber had already raised the waltz from the level of a common dance tune, Chopin was the first to make a special genre of this class of music. He imparted to the waltz, in fact, the dignity of an art form. The fifteen compositions to which he gave the title might just possibly serve for dancing purposes, but, as Schumann said, the dancers should be countesses at least. Ehlert called them 'dances of the soul and not of the body.' But that is not strictly true of all the fifteen. In some the emotional content is certainly the most striking feature, but others have a coquetry which is entirely of the ballroom. The D flat major Waltz (Op. 64, No. 1) is too well known to need more than mention. There is a very silly story which gives the credit of its inception to George Sand, or rather to George Sand's pet dog. The animal was chasing its tail, and Chopin was asked by its mistress to 'set the tail to music.' The result was the D flat Waltz. This story may be coupled with another about the F major Waltz (Op. 34), which relates that during its composition Chopin's cat sprang upon the keyboard, and in its 'feline flight' gave him the idea of the first measures. Chopin had a partiality for the familiar A minor of this same Op. 34. Heller told him one day that this was his favourite, too, and he was so pleased that he invited Heller to luncheon at the Café Riche. Schumann wrote enthusiastically of the Waltz in E flat major (Op. 18); but this was the earliest of the fifteen, published in 1834.

With the exception of the waltzes, the nocturnes are probably the most generally admired of all Chopin's compositions. In many respects they are the most characteristic. For the form he was, of course, indebted to ~~Field~~, but he greatly ennobled it. There is a passion and a grandeur in these nocturnes of Chopin's to which John Field, with all his art in this particular form, never attained. They are true night pieces whose real charm can never be felt amid the glare of electric light in the modern concert-room. One could not imagine anything more exquisitely beautiful in its way for the instrument than the Nocturnes in D flat major (Op. 27, No. 2), E flat major (Op. 9, No. 2) and G major (Op. 37, No. 2): the first for its delicious themes and delicate *fioriture*, the second for its divine melody and sylph-like ornament, the third for its dreaminess and dramatic significance. And yet it was of the E flat Nocturne that Rellstab wrote: 'Where Field smiles Chopin makes a grinning grimace; where Field sighs Chopin groans; where Field shrugs his shoulders Chopin twists his whole body; where Field puts some seasoning into the food Chopin empties a handful of cayenne pepper.' But the finest of all the Chopin nocturnes, to my mind, is the grand C sharp minor (Op. 27, No. 1). Kleczynski sees in it 'a description of a calm night at Venice, where, after a scene of murder, the sea closes over a corpse and continues to serve as a mirror to the moonlight.' This is the way in which Chopin has been sentimentalized by some of his admirers. One prefers to say simply of the magnificent work what Henry T. Finck says of it—namely, that it 'embodies a greater variety of emotion and more genuine dramatic spirit on four pages than many operas on four hundred.' Of the celebrated Nocturne in

C minor (Op. 48, No. 1) very diverse opinions are entertained. Frederick Niecks denies it a foremost place among
the composer's works; Charles Willeby says it is 'sickly
and laboured.' Personally, I agree with James Huneker
that it is among the noblest. Like the C sharp minor just
mentioned, it has the heroic quality. It is broad and
imposing, without a hint of mawkishness, a music drama in
miniature.

It was inevitable that Chopin, who aspired to be his
country's composer, should set the seal of his genius upon
the polonaise and the mazurka, for these are the principal
Polish dances. The polonaise is the court dance *par excellence*.
It expresses, says an authority, 'the national spirit and character
—chivalry, grandeur and stateliness: the cadence with which
each part closes indicates the deep bow of the gentleman and
the graceful curtsy of the lady.' Liszt describes the form as
embodying the noblest traditional feelings of ancient Poland.
In its development everything co-operated which specifically
distinguished the nation from others. 'In the Poles of departed
times manly resolution was united with glowing devotion to
the object of their love. Their knightly heroism was sanc-
tioned by high-soaring dignity, and even the laws of gallantry
and the national costume exerted an influence over the turns
of this dance.'

Thus Liszt, who proceeds to point out that Chopin was
born too late and left his country too early to be initiated into
the original character of the polonaise as danced through his
own observation. But it is difficult to see how he could
have treated the form more successfully than he has done in
these fifteen magnificent compositions.[1] They have a power

[1] There is a sixteenth—in G flat major—but its authenticity is
questioned.

and a splendour entirely their own. Along with the mazurkas, they are the most characteristically Polish of all his works. The Chopin of the popular ideal—the feverish, feminine Chopin of a thousand drawing-rooms—is here; but there is here also a Chopin of the masculine gender, who puts into these energetic rhythms a vigour and a boldness that must arouse the sleepiest indifference. One understands now that remark of Louis Ehlert's that 'Beethoven himself was scarce more vehement and irritable' than this moody Pole on occasion. Love of Poland was in his heart, but hatred of Poland's oppressors was there too. In these polonaises we get both, but the hatred predominates.

The most familiar of the fifteen is the celebrated A major Polonaise (Op. 40, No. 1), known as *Le Militaire.* In this work Rubinstein saw a picture of Poland's greatness. It is the subject of a well-known story. It is said that after composing it in the dreary watches of the night Chopin was terrified by the opening of his door and the entrance of a long train of Polish nobles and ladies, richly robed, who moved slowly past him. Troubled by the ghosts he had raised, the composer, hollow-eyed, rushed from the apartment. This is one of the Carthusian monastery tales, for which there is more foundation than for some of the other legendary nonsense. Another Polonaise—in A flat major (Op. 53)—bears the title of *L'Héroique.* With it, too, an anecdote is associated. When Chopin sat down to play it for the first time the room seemed to fill with the warriors he had evoked (for this is a true war-song), and he fled, terror-struck, before the products of his own imagination. The legend points a moral that need not be specified. The only other Polonaise dignified with a title is the so-called 'Siberian,' or 'Revolt,' in E flat minor (Op. 26, No. 2). This is an awe-inspiring work, a true Siberian picture—fit companion for *L'Héroïque,* with its ring of Damascene blade and silver spur.

The mazurkas are not the best known of Chopin's works, although during his life he published forty-one of these compositions, and fifteen were added after his death. It is needless to say that, as with the polonaise, he took the framework of the form from the national dance, which derives its name, by the way, from the district of Mazovia. Liszt has written eloquently of the form: 'Coquetries, vanities, fantasies, inclinations, elegies, vague emotions, passions, conquests, struggles upon which the safety or favours of others depend, all, all meet in this dance.' The programme is imposing enough, but Chopin has got it all into his mazurkas, and something more. It is a positive miracle how he could write these fifty-six works without in some way repeating himself. As Schumann said, there is something new to be found in each. Lenz described them as Heine's songs on the piano and quoted Liszt as remarking that 'one must harness a new pianist of the first rank to each of them.' Their emotional expression shows Chopin at the two extremes of his temperament, for while some are blithe and joyful others are dark and sorrowful. Some 'dance with the heart, others with the heels.' The best known is the B flat major Mazurka of Op. 7, a 'jolly, reckless composition that makes one happy to be alive and dancing.' The G minor of Op. 24 has fewer technical difficulties than some of the others, and is consequently a favourite. The A flat major of Op. 59 is considered by Sir Henry Hadow to be the most beautiful of them all, but the one in the same key (Op. 50, No. 2) runs it very close. The C major Mazurka (Op. 33, No. 3) is the one connected with the famous anecdote told by Lenz, who was playing it in the presence of Meyerbeer and Chopin. 'Two-four,' exclaimed Meyerbeer at the close. 'Three-four,' answered Chopin testily. 'Let me have it for a ballet in my new opera, and I will show you,' retorted Meyerbeer. 'I tell you it is three-four,' said Chopin, who thereupon played it him-self. Lenz adds, rather unnecessarily, that the composers parted coolly. The Mazurka in F minor (Op. 68, No. 4) has a pathetic interest from the fact that, according to Fontana, it was Chopin's last composition. He wrote it shortly before his death, but was too weak to play it over for himself.

Rubinstein calls the preludes the 'very pearls of his works.' Pleyel paid two thousand francs for them, and they were published in 1839. They are generally supposed to have been written during the visit to Majorca, but some bear internal evidence of an earlier date. Niecks says they consist to a great extent of 'pickings from the composer's folios—of pieces, sketches and memoranda written at various times and kept to be utilized when occasion might offer.' This state-ment could easily be substantiated. Chopin was miserable enough in Majorca, but he wrote febrile and feverish music, such as one finds in the preludes, before he went there. As Kleczynski says: 'People have gone too far in seeking in the preludes for traces of that misanthropy, of that weariness of life to which Chopin was a prey during his stay in the island of Majorca.' Very few of the preludes present this character of ennui, and that which is the most marked, the second, must have been written, according to Count Tarnowski, long before his visit to the Balearic Islands. Several of them are full of humour and gaiety, one at least is strong and energetic; and over all there hovers that spirit of combined sweetness and strength which Schumann so aptly described as 'cannons buried in flowers.' They are 'a sheaf of moods.' To Liszt they were 'types of perfection in a mode created by

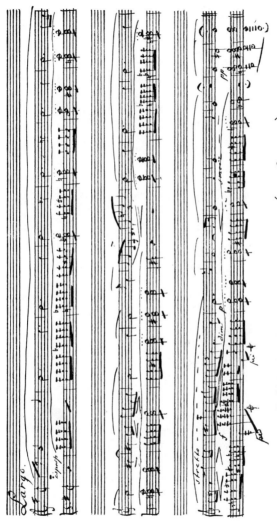

FACSIMILE OF PRELUDE IN E MINOR (OP. 28, NO. 4)

himself and stamped like all his other works with the high impress of his poetic genius.' Ehlert said that none of the other works of Chopin portrayed his inner organization so faithfully and completely. Kullak declared that in their aphoristic brevity they were masterpieces of the first rank. It was of them that Schumann remarked: 'He is the boldest, the proudest poet soul of his time.' One prelude of Chopin, said George Sand in effect, contained more music than all the trumpetings of Meyerbeer. Of the most frequently played, the one in B minor, the same writer says: 'It precipitates the soul into frightful depression.' I will not stop to speak of the others. Take them all in all, these preludes alone would have entitled Chopin to the rank of genius.

The four impromptus have all the usual freedom of this form. They are, indeed, true improvisations, the most remarkable pieces of their kind in existence, not excepting the so-called impromptus of Schubert. The fourth of the series, published posthumously by Fontana, is the well-known *Fantaisie-Impromptu* in C sharp minor (Op. 66). It is frequently heard in our concert halls.

The old idea of the study vanishes in the Etudes of Chopin. The studies of Clementi and Cramer, to take familiar examples, were contrived simply with the view of aiding the student in mastering special mechanical difficulties of the keyboard. Their emotional content was practically *nil.* The studies of Chopin, on the other hand, like those of Liszt, have a twofold purpose. They never lose sight of their main executive aim, but at the same time they seek to give expression to some poetical idea, some musical sentiment, some dramatic situation. In the twenty-seven Studies of Chopin the technical purpose is nearly always clear, though it is never obtrusive. Regarded merely as technical exercises they are admirable. Hans von

Bülow said that he who can play the Study in A flat major (Op. 10, No. 10) in a really finished manner 'may congratulate himself on having climbed to the highest point of the pianist's Parnassus.' Of the D flat major Study (Op. 25, No. 8) the same authority declared that it was the most useful exercise in the whole range of *étude* literature. 'It might,' he remarked, 'be truly called *l'indispensable du pianiste,* if the term, through misuse, had not fallen into disrepute.' It was of certain of these works that Rellstab wrote in 1834: 'Those who have distorted fingers may put them right by practising these studies; but those who have not, should not play them, at least not without having a surgeon at hand.' These were the words of an ignoramus, but they may be taken as sufficiently indicative of the technical value of the Chopin studies. But the technical value, let it be insisted again, is not the full measure of their importance. They serve a very useful purpose in pedagogy, but they are also 'poems fit for Parnassus.' What Schumann said of the second set is true of the whole collection. 'They are all,' he said, 'models of bold, indwelling, creative force, truly poetic creations, not without small blots in their details, but on the whole striking and powerful.' Of the one in G sharp minor (Op. 25, No. 6) Louis Ehlert wrote: 'Chopin not only versifies an exercise in thirds; he transforms it into such a work of art that in studying it one could sooner fancy himself on Parnassus than at a lesson.' Of how many of the studies might not the same thing be said? These works represent, in fact, the entire range of Chopin's genius. They vary in mood just as they vary in mechanism; but there is not one of them that does not show the composer's power of converting even a dry technical exercise into an artistic creation. To deal with them individually is out of the question here. One or two must, however, be singled out for special mention.

Most notable, perhaps, is the Study in C minor, commonly known as 'The Revolutionary' (Op. 10, No. 12). This is said to have been written in Stuttgart in 1831, on the way to Paris, just after Chopin heard of the taking of Warsaw by the Russians. It has been described, and described truly, as 'one of the greatest dramatic outbursts in piano literature.' The composer, says Niecks, seems 'fuming with rage.' Then there is the one in F minor (Op. 10, No. 9), in which Schumann finds 'the song of a sleeping child.'

The A minor (Op. 25, No. 11) has been described by Kullak as 'one of the grandest and most ingenious' of Chopin's Etudes. It is the longest and in every respect the best. Bülow praised it because, 'while producing the greatest fullness of sound imaginable, it keeps itself so entirely and so utterly unorchestral, and represents piano music in the most accurate sense of the word.' And then there is the familiar and oft-played Study in A flat major (Op. 25, No. 1). Here, again, Schumann must be quoted. He says: 'Imagine that an Aeolian harp possessed all the musical scales, and that the hand of an artist were to cause them all to intermingle in all sorts of fantastic embellishments, yet in such a way as to leave everywhere audible a deep fundamental tone and a soft continuously singing upper voice, and you will get the right idea of Chopin's playing.' That was said of Chopin's rendering of this particular Study. But we cannot go over them all. They will surely endure among the classics of the art.

In the four ballades of Chopin we see the composer at his best as a universal artist. He was the first to adapt the name to the form—a name, says the article in Grove's *Dictionary*, which 'seems to be no more specially applicable than that of sonnet is to the pieces which Liszt and others have written under that name.' But 'what's in a name?' Chopin's ballades have less of the Polish tinge than anything else that he wrote, though, strangely enough, more than one of them was suggested by the works of Mickiewicz, the Polish bard. Chopin told Schumann this—that he had been 'incited to the creation of the ballades by the poetry' of his fellow-countryman. Niecks thinks—and I agree with him—that none of Chopin's compositions surpasses his ballades in masterliness of form and beauty and poetry of contents. In them he attains the acme of his power as an artist. In looking at them closely we find that each one differs from the others—that, as Ehlert says, they have but one thing in common—their romantic working-out and the nobility of their motives.

First, we have the G minor Ballade (Op. 23), one of the finest things he ever wrote. Most people have heard the crazy tale of the Englishman who haunted Chopin, beseeching him to teach him this Ballade. The second Ballade, which opens in F major and closes in A minor, is perhaps the most touching of the quartet. Ehlert declared that he had seen children lay aside their games to listen to it. 'It appears,' he said, 'like some fairy tale that has become music. The four-voiced part has such a clearness, it seems as if warm spring breezes were waving the lithe leaves of the palm tree. How soft and sweet a breath steals over the senses and the heart!' This second Ballade was a special favourite of Rubinstein. His 'programme' of the composition may be gathered from the following quotation. 'Is it possible,' he asks, 'that the interpreter does not feel the necessity of representing to his audience a field-flower caught by a gust of wind, a caressing of the flower by the wind; the resistance of the flower, the stormy struggle of the wind; the entreaty of the flower, which at last lies there broken; and paraphrased—the field-flower a rustic maiden, the wind a knight?' Of the Ballade in A flat major what shall be said? It is 'the delight of the schoolgirl, who familiarly toys with its demon, seeing only favour and prettiness in its elegant measures.' In it, said Schumann—it is impossible to get away from him—'in it the refined, gifted Pole, who is accustomed to move in the most distinguished circles of the French capital, is pre-eminently to be recognized.' This composition was suggested by the *Undine* of Mickiewicz. Last of all, there is the Ballade in F minor, dedicated to the Baronne de Rothschild. Here we have Chopin in his most reflective yet lyric mood. It is a fit composition with which to close our survey, for it is Chopin 'at the supreme summit of his art, an art alembicated, personal and intoxicating.'

APPENDICES

APPENDIX A

CALENDAR

(Figures in brackets denote the age reached by the person mentioned during the year in question.)

Year	Age	Life	Contemporary Musicians
1810		Frederic Chopin born, Feb. 22, at Zelazowa Wola, Poland, son of Nicholas Chopin (39), a tutor. The family removes to Warsaw, Oct.	Nicolai born, June 9; Schumann born, June 8. Adam aged 7; Auber 28; Balfe 2; Beethoven 40; Bellini 9; Berlioz 7; Bishop 24; Boieldieu 35; Catel 37; Cherubini 50; Clementi 58; Czerny 19; Donizetti 13; Dussek 49; Field 28; Glinka 7; Gossec 76; Grétry 69; Gyrowetz 47; Halévy 11; Hérold 19; Hummel 32; Kalkbrenner 22; Lesueuer 50; Loewe 14; Marschner 15; Méhul 47; Mendelssohn 1; Mercadante 15; Meyerbeer 19; Onslow 26; Paer 39; Paisiello 69; Pleyel 53; Rossini 18; Salieri 60; Schubert 13; Spontini 36; Spohr 26; Steibelt 45; Vogler 61; Weber 26; Zelter 52.

Year	Age	Life	Contemporary Musicians
1811	1	Second sister, Isabella, born, July 9.	Hiller born, Oct. 24; Liszt born, Oct. 22; Thomas (A.) born, Aug. 5.
1812	2	Nicholas Chopin (41) becomes professor of French at the School of Artillery and Military Engineering in Warsaw.	Dussek (51) dies, March 20; Flotow born, April 27; Thalberg born.
1813	3	Third sister, Emilia, born.	Alkan born, Nov. 30; Dargomizhsky born, Feb. 2/14; Grétry (72) dies, Sept. 24; Macfarren born, March 2; Verdi born, Oct. 10; Wagner born, May 22.
1814	4		Henselt born, May 12; Vogler (65) dies, May 6.
1815	5	Nicholas Chopin (44) adds to his duties the teaching of French at the Military Elementary School.	Franz born, June 28; Heller born, May 15; Kjerulf born, Sept. 15.
1816	6	Begins to take piano lessons from Adalbert Zwyny (60).	Bennett (Sterndale) born, April 13; Paisiello (75) dies, June 5.
1817	7	Plays the piano at a private musical evening and becomes known as a boy prodigy.	Gade born, Feb. 22; Méhul (54) dies, Oct. 18; Monsigny (88) dies, Jan. 14.
1818	8	Plays at a charity concert in Warsaw, Feb. 24, performing a concerto by Gyrowetz (55) and other works. Many invitations to aristocratic houses follow.	Gounod born, June 17; Isouard (43) dies, March 23.

Year	Age	Life	Contemporary Musicians
1819	9		Offenbach born, June 21.
1820	10	Angelica Catalani (40) sings in Warsaw and is so impressed with C. that she presents him with a watch. March dedicated to the Grand Duke Constantine and scored for military band by another hand.	Moniuszko born, May 5; Serov born, Jan. 11/23; Vieuxtemps born, Feb. 20.
1821	11		Elsner (52) founds the Warsaw Conservatoire.
1822	12	Receives lessons in composition from Elsner (53). Composes a Polonaise in G sharp minor (?).	Franck born, Dec. 10; Raff born, May 27.
1823	13	Makes great progress in composition and improvisation.	Kirchner born, Dec. 10; Lalo born, Jan. 27; Reyer born, Dec. 1; Steibelt (58) dies, Sept. 20.
1824	14	Enters the Warsaw Lyceum, where his father is professor of French. Variations on a German Folksong composed.	Bruckner born, Sept. 4; Cornelius born, Dec. 24; Reinecke born, June 23; Smetana born, March 2; Viotti (71) dies, March 3.
1825	15	Plays at two charity concerts at the Conservatoire. Tsar Alexander I (48) hears him and gives him a diamond ring. Rondo, C minor (Op. 1).	Salieri (75) dies, May 7; Strauss (J. ii) born, Oct. 25; Winter (70) dies, Oct. 17.
1826	16	Variations on *Là ci darem* (Op. 2). Holiday at Reinerz, Prussian Silesia, where his sister Emilia (13)	Weber (40) dies, June 4–5.

Year	Age	Life	Contemporary Musicians
		undergoes a cure. His own health is delicate. Holiday finished at his godmother's, Mme Wiesiolowska, at Strzyzewo, and at Antonin, the country seat of Prince Anton Radziwill (51).	
1827	17	Leaves the Warsaw Conservatoire and devotes himself entirely to music. His youngest sister, Emilia (14) dies, April 10. Sonata No. 1, C minor (Op. 4), *Rondo à la Mazur* (Op. 5) and other pieces composed. Piano Trio (Op. 8) begun.	Beethoven (57) dies, March 26.
1828	18	Summer spent at Strzyzewo. Visit to Berlin, Sept. Fantasy on Polish Airs (Op. 13). *Rondo à la Krakowiak,* for piano and orchestra (Op. 14). Rondo for two pianos (Op. 73).	Bargiel born, Oct. 10; Schubert (31) dies, Nov. 19.
1829	19	Meeting with Hummel (51). C. hears Paganini (45). Visit to Vienna, July, where he gives two concerts, Aug. 11 and 18. Visits to Prague, Teplitz and Dresden. Return to Warsaw, Sept. 12. C. falls in love with Konstancja Gladkowska.	Gossec (95) dies, Feb. 16.

Year	Age	Life	Contemporary Musicians
		Second visit to Prince Anton Radziwill (54) at Antonin, where he writes Introduction and Polonaise for piano and cello (Op. 3), Oct. Piano Trio (Op. 8) finished.	
1830	20	First public concert at Warsaw, March 17. He plays the Concerto in F minor (Op. 21). Third concert, Oct. 11, at which Konstancja Gladkowska appears and at which C. plays the Concerto in E minor (Op. 11). C. leaves home, Nov. 1. At Wola, the first station beyond Warsaw, a Cantata, composed for the occasion by Elsner (61), is sung, and he is presented with a goblet filled with Polish earth. With his friend Titus Woyciechowski he visits Breslau, Dresden, Prague and Vienna, where they arrive at the end of Nov.	Catel (57) dies, Nov. 29; Goldmark born, May 18; Rubinstein born, Nov. 16/28.
1831	21	Is less successful in Vienna than before. Has formed a trio with Slawik (25) and Merk (36), and is on friendly terms with Hummel (53) and Thalberg	Pleyel (74) dies, Nov. 14.

Year	Age	Life	Contemporary Musicians
		(19). Departure for Munich, July 20, and concert there, Aug. 28. Visit to Stuttgart, Sept., where he hears of the taking of Warsaw by the Russians. Study in C minor (Op. 10, No. 12) composed. Arrival in Paris, early Oct. C. attends Kalkbrenner's (47) classes without actually taking lessons. Friendship with Liszt (20).	
1832	22	Friendship with Mendelssohn (23), who is in Paris. C.'s first concert, assisted by Baillot (61), Kalkbrenner (48) and others, Feb. 26. Engagements and pupils increase gradually. Meeting with Field (50), Dec. Mazurkas (Opp. 6 and 7) published.	Clementi (80) dies, March 10; Zelter (74) dies, May 15.
1833	23	Becomes a favourite in French and Polish aristocratic circles. C. and Liszt (22) play at a dramatic performance for the benefit of Harriet Smithson (33), April. Meeting with Berlioz (30), to whom she is engaged. Opp. 8–12 published. The last is a set	Brahms born, May 7; Hérold (42) dies, Jan. 19.

Year	Age	Life	Contemporary Musicians
		of Variations on an air by Hérold (42), who died this year. Friendship with Bellini (32), end of year.	
1834	24	Opp. 13–19 published. *Fantaisie Impromptu* (Op. 66) composed. Visit to the Lower Rhenish Musical Festival at Aachen, in Hiller's (23) company, May. Meeting with Mendelssohn (24), with whom they go to Düsseldorf. C. plays at a concert given by Berlioz (31) at the Paris Conservatoire, Dec. 7.	Boieldieu (59) dies, Oct. 8; Borodin born, Oct. 31/Nov. 12; Ponchielli born, Sept. 1.
1835	25	Scherzo No. 1 (Op. 20) published, Feb. *Andante spianato and Polonaise* for piano and orchestra (Op. 22) first performed at a Conservatoire concert, April 26. Visit to Carlsbad to meet his father, July. Visit to Dresden, Sept. He meets Marya Wodzinska (19), a friend of his youth, there, and falls in love with her. Waltz, A flat major (Op. 69, No. 1) composed for her. Visit to Leipzig, where he meets Mendelssohn (26) again, also	Bellini (34) dies, Sept. 24; Cui born, Jan. 6/18; Saint-Saëns born, Oct. 9; Wieniaswki born, July 10.

Appendix A—Calendar

Year	*Age*	*Life*	*Contemporary Musicians*
		Schumann (25) and Clara Wieck (16). Return to Paris by way of Heidelberg, Oct. Op. 24 published, Nov.	
1836	26	Opp. 21–3, 26 and 27 published. Visit to Marienbad, where he meets Marja Wodzinska (20) again and (?) proposes to her. She pledges him to secrecy, uncertain of obtaining her father's consent to a marriage, Aug. Visit to Leipzig, where he meets Schumann (26) again, and return to Paris, Sept. C. shows signs of developing a chest complaint, winter.	Delibes born, Feb. 21.
1837	27	First meeting with George Sand (33), to whom he is introduced by Liszt (26), *c*. Jan. Marja Wodzinska (21) shows by her letters that she does not consider herself engaged to C. Visit to London, July. 12 Studies (Op. 25) published, Oct. Opp. 29–32 published, Dec.	Balakirev born, Jan. 12 (N.S.); Field (55) dies, Jan. 11.
1838	28	Plays at the court of Louis Philippe (65), Feb., and at a concert given by Alkan, March 3. Visit to	Bizet born, Oct. 25; Bruch born, Jan. 6; Schumann (28) dedicates his *Kreisleriana* to C.

207

Year	*Age*	*Life*	*Contemporary Musicians*
		George Sand (34) at Nohant. An intimacy develops between her and C. Opp. 33 and 34 published, Oct. Being delicate in health, C. joins George Sand at Majorca, Nov. Composition of Preludes (Op. 28) and Ballade (Op. 38) progresses.	
1839	29	A wet and miserable winter spent at Valdemosa. C.'s health deteriorates. Preludes (Op. 28) finished and Scherzo (Op. 39) and 2 Polonaises (Op. 40) composed. Return to France, Feb. Spring spent at Marseilles and summer at Nohant. Sonata, B flat minor (Op. 35), composed there. Return to Paris, Oct. 11 Meeting with Moscheles. (45), with whom he appears at court at Saint-Cloud, winter.	Moussorgsky born, March 9/21; Paer (68) dies, May 3; Rheinberger born, March 27.
1840	30	The whole year spent in Paris. Opp. 35–42 published.	Götz born, Dec. 17; Stainer born, June 6; Svendsen born, Sept. 3; Tchaikovsky born, April 25/May 7.
1841	31	Concert given with Laure Cinti-Damoreau (40) and Ernst (27), April 26.	Chabrier born, Jan. 18; Dvořák born, Sept. 8; Pedrell born, Feb. 19.

Appendix A—Calendar

Year	Age	Life	Contemporary Musicians
		Summer once more spent with George Sand (37) at Nohant. Meeting there with Pauline Viardot-Garcia (20). Opp. 43–50 published.	
1842	32	Concert with Viardot-Garcia (21) and Franchomme (34), Feb. 21. At Nohant again in the summer. Delacroix (33) is among the guests.	Boito born, Feb. 24; Cherubini (82) dies, March 15; Massenet born, May 12; Sullivan born, May 13.
1843	33	Another visit to Nohant with George Sand (39), summer. Opp. 51–4 published.	Grieg born, June 15; Sgambati born, May 28.
1844	34	Death of C.'s father, Nicholas Chopin (73) in Poland. Visit to Nohant, summer. Opp. 55 and 56 published.	Rimsky-Korsakov born, March 6/18.
1845	35	Visit to Nohant with George Sand (41), summer. *Berceuse* (Op. 57) and Sonata, B minor (Op. 58), published.	Fauré born, May 13.
1846	36	Summer spent at Nohant. Misunderstandings begin to arise between C. and George Sand (42). Meeting with Matthew Arnold (24), who visits George Sand. Opp. 59–62 published.	

Year	*Age*	*Life*	*Contemporary Musicians*
1847	37	Marriage of George Sand's (43) daughter, Solange Dudevant, to the sculptor Clésinger, May. When C. has returned to Paris, a family quarrel at Nohant causes him to side with Solange, whose mother thereupon breaks with him. His ill-health increases. Opp. 63 – 5 published.	Mackenzie born, Aug. 22; Mendelssohn (38) dies, Nov. 4.
1848	38	C.'s last concert in Paris, Feb. 16. He performs the cello Sonata (Op. 65) with Franchomme (40). Departure for London, April. He plays at many private houses, but his poor health prevents him from accepting all the many invitations he receives. Meeting with Jenny Lind (28), May. C. goes to Scotland with his pupil, Jane Stirling, and stays with her brother-in-law, Lord Torpichen, at Calder House, Aug. He plays at Manchester, Glasgow and Edinburgh, Aug.–Oct. Return to London, *c.* early Nov., worse in health than ever.	Donizetti (51) dies, April 8; Duparc born, Jan. 21; Parry born, Feb. 27.

Year	Age	Life	Contemporary Musicians
		He makes his last public appearance at a Polish ball and concert at the Guildhall, Nov. 16.	
1849	39	Return to Paris from London, Jan. In his critical state of health he is no longer able to teach and play in public. Jane Stirling assists him anonymously with a large sum when he is quite destitute, summer, and Countess Obreskov pays half his rent. His sister, Ludwika Jedrzejewics, comes to nurse him, autumn. Chopin dies in Paris, of laryngeal phthisis, Oct. 17.	Nicolai (39) dies, May 11. Adam aged 46; Alkan 36; Auber 67; Balakirev 13; Balfe 41; Bargiel 21; Bennett (Sterndale) 33; Berlioz 46; Bishop 63; Bizet 11; Boito 7; Borodin 15; Brahms 16; Bruch 11; Bruckner 25; Chabrier 8; Cornelius 25; Cui 14; Czerny 58; Dargomizhsky 36; Delibes 13; Duparc 1; Dvořák 8; Fauré 4; Flotow 37; Franck 27; Franz 34; Gade 32; Glinka 46; Goldmark 19; Gounod 31; Götz 8; Grieg 6; Gyrowetz 86; Halévy 50; Heller 34; Henselt 35; Hiller 38; Kirchner 26; Kjerulf 34; Lalo 26; Liszt 38; Loewe 53; Macfarren 36; Mackenzie 2; Marschner 54; Massenet 7; Mercadante 54; Meyerbeer 58; Moniuszko 29; Moussorgsky 10; Offenbach 30; Onslow 65; Parry 1; Pedrell 8; Ponchielli 15; Raff 27;

Year	*Age*	*Life*	*Contemporary Musicians*
			Reinecke 25; Reyer 26; Rimsky - Korsakov 5; Rheinberger 10; Rossini 57; Rubinstein 19; Saint-Saëns 14; Schumann 39; Serov 29; Sgambati 6; Smetana 25; Spohr 65; Spontini 75; Stainer 9; Strauss (J. ii) 24; Sullivan 7; Svendsen 9; Tchaikovsky 9; Vieuxtemps 29; Wagner 36; Wieniawski 14.

APPENDIX B

CATALOGUE OF WORKS [1]

I. Published with Opus Number during his Lifetime

Op. No.	Date of Publication	Title	Key	Dedication
1	1825	Rondo	C minor	Mme de Linde
2	1830	Variations for piano with orchestral accompaniment, on *Là ci darem la mano*	B flat major	M. Woyciechowski
3	1833	Introduction and Polonaise for piano and cello	C major	M. Joseph Merk
5	1827 (?)	*Rondo à la Mazur*	F major	Mlle la Comtesse Alexandrine de Moriolles
6	1832	4 Mazurkas	F sharp minor C sharp minor E major E flat minor	Mlle la Comtesse Pauline Plater
7	1832	5 Mazurkas	B flat major A minor F minor A flat major C major	M. Johns

[1] All for piano solo unless otherwise mentioned.

Op. No.	Date of Publi-cation	Title	Key	Dedication
8	1833	Trio for piano, violin and cello	G minor	Prince Antoine Radziwill
9	1833	3 Nocturnes	B flat minor E flat major B major	Mme Camille Pleyel
10	1833	12 Grand Studies	C major A minor E major C sharp minor G flat major E flat minor C major F major F minor A flat major E flat major C minor	M. Franz Liszt
11	1833	Concerto No. 1 for piano and orchestra	E minor	M. Fr. Kalk-brenner
12	1833	Variations on the favourite Rondo from Hérold's *Ludovic*, 'Je vends des scapulaires'	B flat major	Mlle Emma Horsford
13	1834	Grand Fantasy on Polish Airs for piano & orchestra	A major	M. J. P. Pixis
14	1834	*Krakowiak*, Grand Concert Rondo for piano and or-chestra	F major	Mme la Prin-cesse Adam Czartoryska

Op. No.	Date of Publication	Title	Key	Dedication
15	1834	3 Nocturnes	F major F sharp major G minor	M. Ferdinand Hiller
16	1834	Rondo	E flat major	Mlle Caroline Hartmann
17	1834	4 Mazurkas	B flat major E minor A flat major A minor	Mme Lina Freppa
18	1834	Grand Waltz	E flat major	Mlle Laura Horsford
19	1834	*Bolero*	C major	Mme la Comtesse E. de Flahault
20	1834	Scherzo No. 1	B minor	M. T. Albrecht
21	1836	Concerto No. 2 for piano and orchestra	F minor	Mme la Comtesse Delphine Potocka
22	1836	*Andante spianato et Polonaise brillante*	E flat major	Mme la Baronne d'Est
23	1836	Ballade No. 1	G minor	Baron Stockhausen
24	1835	4 Mazurkas	G minor C major A flat major B minor	M. le Comte de Perthuis
25	1837	12 Studies	A flat major F minor F major A minor E minor G sharp minor	Mme la Comtesse d'Agoult

Chopin

Op. No.	Date of Publication	Title	Key	Dedication
			C sharp minor	
			D flat major	
			G flat major	
			B minor	
			A minor	
			C minor	
26	1836	2 Polonaises	C sharp minor	Mr. J. Dessauer
			E flat minor	
27	1836	2 Nocturnes	C sharp minor	Mme la Comtesse d'Apponyi
			D flat major	
28	1839	24 Preludes	—	French edition to M. Camille Pleyel; German edition to Mr. J. C. Kessler
29	1837	Impromptu No. 1	A flat major	Mlle la Comtesse le Lobau
30	1837	4 Mazurkas	C minor	Mme la Princesse de Württemberg, née Princesse Czartoryska
			B minor	
			D flat major	
			C sharp minor	
31	1837	Scherzo No. 2	B flat minor	Mlle la Comtesse Adèle de Fürstenstein
32	1837	2 Nocturnes	B major	Mme la Baronne de Billing
			A flat major	
33	1838	4 Mazurkas	G sharp minor	Mlle la Comtesse Mostowska
			D major	
			C major	
			B minor	
34	1838	3 *Valses brillantes*	A flat major	Mlle de Thun-Hohenstein

Appendix B—Catalogue of Works

Op. No.	Date of Publi- cation	Title	Key	Dedication
			A minor	Mme. G. d'Ivri
			F major	Mlle A. d'Eich- thal
35	1840	Sonata	B flat minor	—
36	1840	Impromptu No. 2	F sharp minor	—
37	1840	2 Nocturnes	G minor	—
			G major	
38	1840	Ballade No. 2	F major	Mr. R. Schu- mann
39	1840	Scherzo No. 3	C sharp minor	M.A.Gutmann
40	1840	2 Polonaises	A major	M. J. Fontana
			C minor	
41	1840	4 Mazurkas	C sharp minor	M. E. Witwicki
			E minor	
			B major	
			A flat major	
42	1840	Waltz	A flat major	—
43	1841	*Tarantella*	A flat major	—
44	1841	Polonaise	F sharp minor	Mme la Prin- cesse Charles de Beauvau
45	1841	Prelude	C sharp minor	Mlle la Prin- cesse E. Czer- nicheff
46	1841	Concert Allegro	A major	Mlle F. Müller
47	1841	Ballade No. 3	A flat major	Mlle P. de Noailles
48	1841	2 Nocturnes	C minor	Mlle L. Duperré
			F sharp minor	
49	1841	Fantasy	F minor	Mme la Prin- cesse C. de Souzzo

Op. No.	Date of Publication	Title	Key	Dedication
50	1841	3 Mazurkas	G major A flat major C sharp minor	M. Léon Szmitkowski
51	1843	Impromptu No. 3	G flat major	Mme la Comtesse Esterházy
52	1843	Ballade No. 4	F minor	Mme la Baronne C. de Rothschild
53	1843	Polonaise	A flat major	M. A. Leo
54	1843	Scherzo No. 4	E major	Mlle J. de Caraman
55	1844	2 Nocturnes	F minor E flat major	Mlle. J. M. Stirling
56	1844	3 Mazurkas	B major C major C minor	Mlle C. Maberly
57	1845	*Berceuse*	D flat major	Mlle Elise Gavard
58	1845	Sonata	B minor	Mme la Comtesse E. de Perthuis
59	1846	3 Mazurkas	A minor A flat major F sharp minor	—
60	1846	*Barcarolle*	F sharp major	Mme la Baronne Stockhausen
61	1846	*Polonaise-Fantaisie*	A flat major	Mme A. Veyret
62	1846	2 Nocturnes	B major E major	Mlle R. de Könneritz
63	1847	3 Mazurkas	B major F minor C sharp minor	Mme la Comtesse Czosnowska

Appendix B—Catalogue of Works

Op. No.	Date of Publication	Title	Key	Dedication
64	1847	3 Waltzes	D flat major	Mme la Comtesse Potocka
			C sharp minor	Mme la Baronne de Rothschild
			A flat major	Mme la Baronne Bronicka
65	1847	Sonata for piano and cello	G minor	M. A. Franchomme

II. PUBLISHED WITHOUT OPUS NUMBER DURING HIS LIFETIME

Date	Title	Key
1833	*Grand Duo Concertant* for piano and cello on theme from *Robert le Diable*, composed with Franchomme	E major
1840	3 Studies for the *Méthode des Méthodes* of Moscheles and Fétis	F minor A flat major D flat major
1841	Variations on the March from Bellini's *I Puritani*	E major
1842	Mazurka for an album, *Notre Temps*, published by Schott	A minor

III. PUBLISHED POSTHUMOUSLY WITH OPUS NUMBER

Op. No.	Date of Composition	Date of Publication	Title	Key
4	1827	1851	Sonata [1]	C minor
66	1834	1855	*Fantaisie-Impromptu*	C sharp minor

[1] Dedicated to Joseph Elsner

Op. No.	Date of Composition	Date of Publication	Title	Key
67	1835	1855	4 Mazurkas	G major
	1849	,,		G minor
	1835	,,		C major
	1846	,,		A minor
68	1830	1855	4 Mazurkas	C major
	1827	,,		A minor
	1830	,,		F major
	1849	,,		F minor
69	1836	1855	2 Waltzes	A flat major
	1829	,,		B minor
70	1835	1855	3 Waltzes	G flat major
	1843	,,		F minor
	1830	,,		D flat major
71	1827	1855	3 Polonaises	D minor
	1828	,,		B flat major
	1829	,,		F minor
72	1827	1855	Nocturne	E minor
	1829		*Marche funèbre*	C minor
	1830		3 Ecossaises	D major, G major, and D flat major
73	1828	1855	Rondo for two pianos	C major
74	1829–47	1855	17 Polish Songs for voice and piano	

Appendix B—Catalogue of Works

Date of Composition	Date of Publication	Title	Key
1824	1851	Variations on a German Air	E major
1825	—	Mazurka	G major
1825	—	Do.	B flat major
1829–30	—	Do.	D major
1832	—	A remodelling of the preceding Mazurka	D major
1833	—	Mazurka	C major
—	—	Do.	A minor
—	1868	Waltz	E minor
1822	1864	Polonaise	G sharp minor
1822	1872	Polonaise [of doubtful authenticity]	G flat major
1826	—	Polonaise	B flat major
1829	—	Waltz	E major
—	1918	Prelude (published in Geneva)	
—	—	Fugue	
—	—	Nocturne	
1829 (?)	—	*Souvenir de Paganini*	A major

APPENDIX C

Alard, Delphin (1815–88), French violinist and composer for his instrument, student at the Paris Conservatoire, where he succeeded Baillot (q.v.) as professor.

Alboni, Marietta (1823–94), Italian contralto singer, pupil of Rossini, made her first appearance in 1843, at the Scala in Milan. Sang with much success in Paris and London.

Baillot, Pierre Marie François de Sales (1771–1842), French violinist, studied in Rome and later under Catel, Cherubini and Reicha in Paris; joined Napoleon's private band in 1802 and began to give chamber concerts in 1814. He was professor at the Conservatoire and composed works for his instrument and chamber music.

Catalani, Angelica (1780–1849), Italian soprano singer, made her first appearance at the Fenice Theatre, Venice, in 1795. Went to Portugal in 1804, to London in 1806 and became manager of the Italian Opera in Paris in 1813.

Chorley, Henry Fothergill (1808–72), English music critic and author, contributor to the *Athenæum* from 1830.

Cinti-Damoreau, Laure (1801–63), French opera singer, student at the Paris Conservatoire. Made her first appearance at the Théâtre Italien at the age of eighteen and at the Opéra in 1826. She remained there until 1835 and the following year joined the Opéra-Comique. Rossini and Auber wrote parts for her.

Czerny, Karl (1791–1857), pianist and composer in Vienna, pupil of Beethoven, Hummel and Clementi, teacher of Liszt. Wrote vast quantities of music, mainly instructive works for his instrument.

Davison, James William (1813–85), English writer on music, critic of *The Times*, 1846–79, editor of *The Musical World*, husband of the pianist Arabella Goddard.

Appendix C—Personalia

Dorn, Heinrich (1804–92), German composer, teacher and conductor, pupil of Zelter in Berlin, teacher of Schumann in Leipzig, opera conductor in Hamburg and Riga, where he succeeded Wagner in 1839. Finally conductor at the Royal Opera and professor in Berlin.

Dorus, Julie Aimée Josèphe (1805–96), French opera singer, student at the Paris Conservatoire and pupil of Paer (q.v.). Made her first appearance at the Opéra in 1830, where she succeeded Cinti-Damoreau (q.v.) in the principal parts in 1835. Married the violinist Gras in 1833.

Dotzauer, Justus Johann Friedrich (1783–1860), German violoncellist, first in the court orchestra at Meiningen, then in Leipzig, Berlin and Dresden, where he remained until his retirement in 1852. He composed an opera, a symphony, chamber music and many works for his instrument.

Dussek, Jan Ladislav (1761–1812), Czech pianist and composer whose works marked a great advance in pianoforte, as distinct from harpsichord, style.

Elsner, Joseph Xaver (1769–1854), Polish composer, first director of the Warsaw Conservatoire, founded in 1821. Wrote twenty-two Polish operas and numerous other works.

Ernst, Heinrich Wilhelm (1814–65), Moravian violinist and composer for his instrument, pupil of Böhm, Seyfried (q.v.) and Mayseder (q.v.) in Vienna. Lived in Paris for six years and afterwards travelled much.

Falcon, Marie Cornélie (1814–97), French soprano singer, student at the Paris Conservatoire and pupil of Nourrit (q.v.) for operatic acting. Made her first appearance in 1832, at the Opéra.

Fétis, François Joseph (1784–1871), French musicologist, appointed professor at the Paris Conservatoire in 1821 and librarian in 1827. Author of a *Biographie universelle des musiciens,* a *Histoire générale de la musique* and many theoretical works.

Franchomme, Auguste Joseph (1808–84), French violoncellist, in the orchestra first of the Paris Opéra, then of the Théâtre Italien. Member of Alard's (q.v.) quartet.

Göhringer, Franzilla (born 1816), German mezzo-soprano singer, adopted daughter and pupil of Pixis (q.v.), with whom she went on tour in 1833. At Naples Pacini wrote the title part of the opera *Saffo* for her. She married an Italian named Minofrio.

Grisi, Giulia (1811–69), Italian opera singer, made her first appearance at the age of seventeen. Bellini wrote the part of Adalgisa in *Norma* for her. She first went to Paris in 1832 and to London in 1834. She married Mario (q.v.).

Gutmann, Adolf (1819–82), German pianist and composer for his instrument, pupil of Chopin in Paris.

Gyrowetz, Adalbert (1763–1850), Bohemian composer, prolific writer of orchestral, operatic and chamber music.

Habeneck, François Antoine (1781–1849), French violinist, conductor and composer, pupil of Baillot at the Paris Conservatoire, where he was afterwards professor and conductor of the orchestra.

Hallé, Charles (Carl Halle) (1819–95), German pianist and conductor, settled in Paris from 1836 and in England after the Revolution of 1848. Founded the Hallé Orchestra at Manchester in 1857.

Heinefetter, Clara (1816–57), German singer, engaged for several years at the Opera in Vienna.

Herz, Henri (Heinrich) (1806?–88), Austrian pianist and composer for his instrument, settled in Paris.

Herz, Jacob Simon (1794–1880), brother of the preceding, teacher of the piano and minor composer.

Hesse, Adolf Friedrich (1809–63), German organist and composer at Breslau.

Hiller, Ferdinand (1811–85), German pianist and composer, pupil of Hummel, settled in Paris 1828–35, later at Frankfort, Leipzig and Dresden.

Kalkbrenner, Friedrich Wilhelm Michael (1788–1849), German pianist and composer for his instrument, settled in Paris.

Klengel, August Alexander (1783–1852), German organist and composer, pupil of Clementi, appointed court organist at Dresden in 1816.

Appendix C—Personalia

Kreutzer, Conradin (1780–1849), German composer and conductor, holding various appointments, mainly in Vienna. Composed many operas, including *Das Nachtlager von Granada.*

Kummer, Friedrich August (1797–1879), German violoncellist and composer for his instrument, living most of his life in Dresden.

Lablache, Luigi (1794–1858), Italian bass singer, made his first stage appearance at the Teatro San Carlino in Naples and later became famous all over Europe.

Lachner, Franz (1803–90), German composer and conductor, student in Vienna and friend of Schubert, later conductor of the Kärnthnerthor Theatre there.

Lanner, Joseph Franz Karl (1801–43), Viennese composer of dance music, second only to Johann Strauss, jun.

Lefébure-Wély, Louis James Alfred (1817–70), French organist and composer, student at the Paris Conservatoire and organist at the Madeleine 1847–58.

Lesueur, Jean François (1760–1837), French composer and theorist, professor of composition at the Paris Conservatoire from 1818.

Levasseur, Nicholas Prosper (1791–1871), French bass singer, made his first appearance, at the Paris Opéra, in 1813.

Lipinski, Karl Joseph (1790–1861), Polish violinist, travelled much and became leader of the court orchestra at Dresden in 1839.

Lysberg, Charles Samuel (1821–73), Swiss pianist and composer for his instrument, pupil of Chopin in Paris.

Malibran, Maria Felicità (1808–36), Spanish soprano singer, daughter of Manuel Garcia, whose pupil she was. She made her stage appearance in London in 1825. Married Malibran in 1826 but, the match being unhappy, lived with Bériot from 1830, marrying him, after a protracted divorce, six months before her death.

Mario, Giovanni Matteo, Cavaliere di Candia (1810–83), Italian tenor singer, made his first appearance, in Paris, 1838. The following year he paid his first visit to London. He married Grisi (q.v.).

Mayseder, Joseph (1789–1863), Austrian violinist and composer, made his first appearance, in Vienna, 1800, and afterwards came to hold several important appointments.

Merk, Joseph (1795–1852), Austrian violoncellist, leader of the Opera orchestra in Vienna from 1818 and professor at the Conservatorium from 1823. He composed much for his instrument.

Morlacchi, Francesco (1784–1841), Italian composer and conductor, pupil of Zingarelli and Mattei. Produced many operas in Italy and was appointed musical director to the Saxon court at Dresden in 1810.

Moscheles, Ignaz (1794–1870), Bohemian pianist and composer, studied in Prague and Vienna, later travelled a great deal and lived much in Paris and London.

Nourrit, Adolphe (1802–39), French tenor singer, made his first appearance, at the Paris Opéra, in 1821, remaining attached to that theatre for sixteen years.

Onslow, George (1784–1853), Anglo-French composer living alternately in Paris and at his estate at Clermont-Ferrand. He wrote three comic operas and many other works, including a great deal of chamber music.

Osborne, George Alexander (1806–93), Irish pianist and composer for his instrument, pupil of Pixis (q.v.) and Kalkbrenner (q.v.) in Paris, settled in London in 1843.

Paer, Ferdinando (1771–1839), Italian opera composer, appointed *maestro di cappella* at Venice in 1791, afterwards settled successively in Vienna, Dresden and Paris.

Pasta, Giuditta (1798–1865), Italian opera singer, studied in Paris, made her first appearance in 1815 and went to London in 1816. In Paris she was first heard at the Théâtre Italien in 1821.

Pixis, Johann Peter (1788–1874), German pianist and composer for his instrument, settled in Paris in 1825 and at Baden-Baden in 1845.

Pleyel, Camille (1788–1855), piano maker, music publisher and pianist in Paris, son of Ignaz Pleyel (1757–1831).

Prudent, Emile Racine Gauthier (1817–63), pianist and composer in Paris.

Appendix C—Personalia

Radziwill, Anton, Prince (1775–1833), Polish amateur musician, composer and violoncellist. His chief work is incidental music to Goethe's *Faust*.

Réber, Napoléon-Henri (1807–80), French composer, pupil of Lesueur (q.v.), appointed professor of harmony at the Paris Conservatoire in 1851 and of composition in 1862.

Reicha, Anton (1770–1836), German composer at Bonn and Vienna, later in Paris, where he succeeded Méhul at the Conservatoire in 1817.

Rellstab, Heinrich Friedrich Ludwig (1799–1860), writer on music in Berlin, appointed critic to the *Vossische Zeitung* in 1826.

Richards, Henry Brinley (1817–85), Welsh pianist and composer settled in London after having been a pupil of Chopin in Paris. Composer of *God bless the Prince of Wales*.

Ries, Ferdinand (1784 -1838), German pianist and composer, pupil of Beethoven.

Roger, Gustave Hippolite (1815–79), French tenor singer, student at the Paris Conservatoire, made his first appearance, at the Opéra-Comique, in 1838.

Rolla, Antonio (1798–1837), Italian violinist and composer for his instrument, leader of the Italian Opera orchestra at Dresden 1823–35, son of Alessandro Rolla (1757–1841).

Rubini, Giovanni Battista (1795–1854), Italian tenor singer, first appeared at Pavia, went to Paris for the first time in 1825 and to London in 1831.

Schmitt, Aloys (1788–1866), German pianist and teacher living by turns at Frankfort, Berlin and Hanover, master of Hiller (q.v.).

Schnabel, Joseph Ignaz (1767–1831), organist and teacher of singing at Breslau.

Schroeder-Devrient, Wilhelmine (1804–60), German soprano singer, studied in Vienna, where she made her first appearance in 1821.

Schulhoff, Julius (1825–98), Bohemian pianist and drawing-room composer, settled in Paris from 1842 until the 1848 Revolution, then touring, and finally living at Dresden and Berlin.

Schuppanzigh, Ignaz (1776–1830), violinist and director of the

Augarten concerts in Vienna. Gave Beethoven violin lessons in 1794 and was the first to lead his string quartets.

Seyfried, Ignaz Xaver (1776–1841), composer in Vienna, pupil of Kozeluch and Haydn, conductor at the Theater an der Wien 1801–26, wrote countless works for the stage, much church music and some theoretical works.

Sontag, Henriette (1806–54), German soprano singer, student at the Conservatoire of Prague, where she appeared at short notice at the Opera at the age of fifteen. Afterwards appeared and studied in Vienna, first went to Paris in 1826 and to London in 1828.

Stamaty, Camille Marie (1811–70), composer and teacher of Greek extraction, born in Rome but settled in Paris from childhood.

Tamburini, Antonio (1800–76), Italian baritone singer, was first taught the horn, but appeared in opera at the age of eighteen, at Bologna. First appeared in London and Paris in 1832.

Tellefsen, Thomas Dyke Acland (1823–74), Norwegian pianist, pupil of Chopin, with whom he came to England in 1848.

Thalberg, Sigismund (1812–71), German pianist and composer for his instrument, studied under Hummel and Sechter in Vienna and made his first public appearance there in 1826.

Viardot-Garcia, Pauline (1821–1910), Spanish operatic singer, daughter of Manuel Garcia and sister of Malibran (q.v.), studied piano as well as singing and made her first appearance as a vocalist in 1837, in Brussels. In 1839 she paid her first visit to London.

Zelter, Carl Friedrich (1758–1832), composer, conductor and teacher in Berlin, friend of Goethe and teacher of Mendelssohn. Conductor of the Singakademie.

APPENDIX D

BIBLIOGRAPHY

Audley, Mme A., 'Frédéric Chopin, sa vie et ses œuvres.' (Paris, 1880.)

Barbedette, H., 'F. Chopin: Essai de critique musicale.' (Paris, 1869.)

Bidou, Henri, 'Chopin.' Translated by Catherine Alison Phillips. (London, 1927.)

Bie, Oscar, 'A History of the Pianoforte and Pianoforte Players. (London, 1901.)

Binental, Léopold, 'Chopin' (in Polish). (Warsaw, 1930.)
—— 'Chopin' (in German). (Leipzig, 1932.)
—— 'Chopin' (in French). (Paris, 1934.)

Chopin, Frederic, Letters. Collected by Henryk Opienski. Translated by E. L. Voynich. (London, 1932.)

Finck, Henry T., 'Chopin and other Musical Essays.' (New York, 1899.)

Ganche, Edouard, 'Dans le souvenir de Frédéric Chopin.' (Paris, 1925.)
—— 'Frédéric Chopin: sa vie et ses œuvres.' (Paris, 1921.)
—— 'La Pologne et F. Chopin.' (Paris, 1918.)
—— 'Voyages avec Frédéric Chopin.' (Paris, 1934.)

Hadow, W. H., 'Studies in Modern Music,' vol. ii. (London, 1926.)

Hallé, C. E. and Marie, 'The Life and Letters of Sir Charles Hallé.' (London, 1896.)

Haweis, H. R., 'Music and Morals.' (London, 1876.)

Hervey, Arthur, 'French Music in the Nineteenth Century.' (London, 1903.)

Chopin

Hoesick, Ferdynand, 'Chopin' (in Polish). 3 vols. (Warsaw and Cracow, 1911.)

Hueffer, Francis, 'Musical Studies.' (Edinburgh, 1880.)

Huneker, James, 'Chopin: the Man and his Music.' (London, 1903.)

Jachimecki, Zdilas, 'Frédéric Chopin et son œuvre.' (Paris, 1930.)

Jonson, E. G. Ashton, 'Handbook to Chopin's Works.' (London.)

Karasowski, Moritz, 'Life and Letters of Frederic Chopin.' Translated by Emily Hill. 2 vols. (London, 1879.)

Karlowicz, Mieczyslaw, 'Souvenirs inédits de Fr. Chopin.' (Paris, 1904.)

Kelley, Edgar Stillman, 'Chopin, the Composer.' (New York, 1913.)

Kleczynski, Jan, 'Frédéric Chopin: de l'Interprétation de ses œuvres.' (Paris, 1880) English translation by A. Whittingham. (London.)

—— 'Chopin's Greater Works.' Translated, with additions, by Natalie Janotha. (London, 1896.)

Kuhe, Wilhelm, 'My Musical Recollections.' (London, 1896.)

Leichtentritt, Hugo, 'Analyse der Chopinschen Klavierwerke.' (Berlin, 1921.)

—— 'Fr. Chopin' (in German). (Berlin, 1905.)

Lenz, W. de, 'The Great Piano Virtuosos of our Time.' Translated by R. Baker. (London.)

Liszt, Franz, 'Life of Chopin.' Translated by John Broadhouse. (London.)

Maine, Basil, 'Chopin.' (London, 1933.)

Mariotti, Giovanni, 'Chopin' (in Italian). (Florence, 1933.)

Murdoch, William, 'Chopin: his Life.' (London, 1934.)

Niecks, Frederick, 'Frederic Chopin as Man and Musician.' 2 vols. (London, 1888.)

Opienski, Henryk, 'Chopin' (in Polish). (1910.)

Paderewski, Ignace, 'Chopin—a Discourse.' Translated by Laurence Alma-Tadema. (London, 1911.)

Page, B. P., 'Chopin.' (London, 1925.)

Appendix D—Bibliography

Poirée, Elie, 'Chopin.' (Paris, 1907.)

Pourtalès, Guy de, 'Frederick Chopin: the Man of Solitude.' Translated by Charles Bayly, jun. (London, 1930.)

Przybyszewski, Stanislaw, 'Zur Psychologie des Individuums: Chopin und Nietzsche.' (Berlin, 1892.)

Scharlitt, Bernhard, 'Chopin' (in German). (Leipzig, 1919.)

—— 'Friedrich Chopins gesammelte Briefe.' (Leipzig, 1911.)

Schucht, J., 'Friedrich Chopin und seine Werke.' (Leipzig.)

Schumann, Robert, 'Music and Musicians.' Translated by Fanny Raymond Ritter. (London, 1891.)

Shedlock, J. S., 'The Pianoforte Sonata.' (London, 1895.)

Sowinski, Albert, 'Les Musiciens Polonais.' (Paris, 1874.)

Tarnowski, Count, 'Chopin.' Translated by Natalie Janotha. (London, *Musical Courier,* July–Sept. 1899.)

Uminska and Kennedy, 'Chopin, the Child and the Lad.' (London, 1925.)

Valetta, Ippolito, 'Chopin: la vita, le opere.' (Turin, 1910.)

Vuillermoz, Emile, 'La Vie amoureuse de Chopin.' (Paris, 1927.)

Weissmann, Adolf, 'Chopin' (in German). (Berlin, 1912.)

Willeby, Charles, 'Frederic François Chopin.' (London, 1892.)

Wodzinski, Count, 'Les Trois Romans de Frédéric Chopin.' (Paris, 1886.)

Interesting matter will also be found, incidentally, in the letters and diaries of Berlioz, Delacroix, Henselt, Hiller, Mendelssohn, Moscheles, Rubinstein, Schumann and others.

For the George Sand question reference may be made to *George Sand* by Bertha Thomas, 'George Sand' by Matthew Arnold (in *Mixed Essays*), *Portraits contemporains* by Sainte-Beuve, *French Poets and Novelists* by Henry James, and George Sand's own *Correspondance, Histoire de ma vie, Un Hiver à Majorque, Lucrezia Floriani* and *Elle et lui.* Something may also be gathered from Heine's *Lutetia,* from Zola's *Documents littéraires* and from the *Journal des Goncourt.*

INDEX

Index

Index